OTHER BOOKS BY
DR. SAMUEL WHITE, III

CARING FOR YOUR SOUL: Improving your life

HEALING YOUR SOUL: Christian Self-Care

IT IS WELL WITH MY SOUL: Spiritual Care for the Dying

DYING IN PEACE: Preparing for Eternity

MY BROTHERS KEEPER: Church Ministry for Young African American Males

CAPITALIST CHRISTIAN CONTRADICTION: God Against Greed

NO MORE TEARS: Comfort for the Grieving

HEALING YOUR GRIEF

All books are available online and website drsamuelwhite.com

ENDORSEMENTS

"Rev. White has crafted a valuable guide for helping caregivers learn how to engage in meaningful spiritual dialogue with aging adults, so they may reflect on their life and purpose."
    Mary Kummer Naber, President/CEO
    PACE Southeast Michigan

"Dr. White's contribution will serve as a welcome reference resource to those dedicated to the loving care of the elderly. The author's holistic approach provides multi-layered helps that will empower caregivers to provide meaningful care and support. The focus on the oft-neglected self-care of the caregiver is welcomed and strategically highlighted."
    Rev. Dr. Kenneth E. Harris, President, Ecumenical Theological Seminary, Senior Pastor, Detroit Bible Tabernacle

"There is no doubt that this book will impact all who read it whether an aging adult, personal caregiver or the healthcare providers who have chosen caring for this population as their calling. This book helps us see and understand the impact that spirituality and religion have on the quality of life of an aging population." – Gwen Graddy, MD, Chief Executive Officer of PACE SEMI

"Dr. White skillfully and succinctly describes the existential needs of the elderly in this simple, but spectacular read. Summarizing empirical research, quotes from the brilliant, vast personal experience, and alliterative aids, he provides a comprehensive guide for primary spiritual care for both families and professional caregivers." – Evan Fonger, MD, PACE SEMI, Rivertown

"As a social worker for PACE, I highly recommend this book to my co-workers, friends and family members who work in the health care industry. This is an excellent resource for all who work for nursing homes, assistant living, hospice, and other organizations who care for seniors." – Linda Bazzy, LMSW, PACE SEMI

"Dr. Samuel White, III has authored a comprehensive yet practical handbook for health care professionals and even family members caring for aging adults. I highly recommend, *Aging Gracefully, Spiritual Care for Aging Adults* for those interested in deepening their understanding of 'spiritual growth' in the elderly and incorporating this in their practice, caring for the whole person -mind, body and spirit." – Sue Hammel, RN, BSN, PACE Southeast Michigan, Director of Operations-West

"*Aging Gracefully, Spiritual Care for Aging Adults* tells how a positive spiritual and or religious attitude can enhance the aging process and when it is shared with a support group." – Maxine McBride, Coordinator Friendship Baptist Church Senior/Retiree Program

Aging Gracefully

SPIRITUAL CARE FOR AGING ADULTS

Dr. Samuel White, III

WESTBOW
PRESS®
A DIVISION OF THOMAS NELSON
& ZONDERVAN

Copyright © 2018 Dr. Samuel White, III.

All rights reserved. No part of this book may be used or reproduced by any means, graphic, electronic, or mechanical, including photocopying, recording, taping or by any information storage retrieval system without the written permission of the author except in the case of brief quotations embodied in critical articles and reviews.

WestBow Press books may be ordered through booksellers or by contacting:

WestBow Press
A Division of Thomas Nelson & Zondervan
1663 Liberty Drive
Bloomington, IN 47403
www.westbowpress.com
1 (866) 928-1240

Because of the dynamic nature of the Internet, any web addresses or links contained in this book may have changed since publication and may no longer be valid. The views expressed in this work are solely those of the author and do not necessarily reflect the views of the publisher, and the publisher hereby disclaims any responsibility for them.

Any people depicted in stock imagery provided by Getty Images are models, and such images are being used for illustrative purposes only.
Certain stock imagery © Getty Images.

Scripture quotations are from New Revised Standard Version Bible, copyright © 1989 National Council of the Churches of Christ in the United States of America. Used by permission. All rights reserved.

Scripture taken from the King James Version of the Bible

ISBN: 978-1-9736-2640-4 (sc)
ISBN: 978-1-9736-2642-8 (hc)
ISBN: 978-1-9736-2641-1 (e)

Library of Congress Control Number: 2018904659

Print information available on the last page.

WestBow Press rev. date: 01/20/2020

This book is dedicated to my beautiful sisters Dee Ann, Cherise, and Renee who provide the daily care for our 84-year-old mother who is aging gracefully. Also, this book is dedicated to every health aide, Pastor, Chaplain, Deacon, Nurse, Social Worker, secretary, Recreational therapist, Physician, Administrator, dietician, geriatric worker and caregiver who loves and cares for the elderly.

*TO MY LORD AND SAVIOR JESUS CHRIST
WHO HAS BLESSED ME TO AGE GRACEFULLY*

"Love, Laugh, Learn and eat your dessert first"- **Anna White**

TO
MY DEAR MOTHER ANNA MAE WHITE
WHO IS AGING GRACEFULLY
AND
WILL NOT GO GENTLE INTO THAT GOOD NIGHT

Contents

Preface xvii
Acknowledgments xix
Introduction xxi

Chapter 1   Spirituality of Aging Adults 1
Chapter 2   Spiritual Assessment of Aging Adults 11
Chapter 3   Spiritual Care for Aging Adults 26
Chapter 4   Spiritual Care Support Group for Aging Adults 49
Chapter 5   Spiritual Values for Aging Adults 69
Chapter 6   Spiritual Self-Care for Caregivers and
            Healthcare Providers 75

Notes 83
Bibliography 85
Index 88
Appendix 1   Multidimensional Spiritual Assessment 89
Appendix 2   Spiritual Care Needs Of Aging Adults 91
Appendix 3   Different Religious Beliefs And Practices 93
Appendix 4   Spiritual Care Plan 99
Appendix 5   Spiritual Care for Persons with Dementia 101
Appendix 6   Aging Gracefully Session 109

Preface

Where has the time gone? It seemed like only yesterday when I was slim, trim, with a pep in my step and a glide in my stride. Now, I am heavier, slower and forget to carry my AARP card. I can remember playing basketball with my children and letting them win. Now, I get tired just watching and playing video basketball games that my son lets me win. Time has brought about a change. Hopefully, I can change and grow gracefully like my grandfather.

He was a sixty-five-year-old African American, who stood 5 feet 5, had a medium build, silver hair and wore round glasses. He had a pleasant, peaceful disposition and played his guitar and sang with great passion. He was my maternal grandfather Henry Shields and he aged gracefully.

My grandfather formed a gospel band called, The *Gospelaires* and they would visit various Nursing Homes in Rochester N.Y. singing gospels and hymns. Occasionally he allowed me to come with him and preach. I was a young seminarian and had more zeal than knowledge. I did not preach well, and I do not think I impressed anyone. However, I was impressed by my 65-year-old grandfather's passion to serve His peers. I can still visualize him playing his guitar singing, *"He Touched Me"*. He sang with his heart and soul.

Forty years later, I share my late Grandfathers passion to serve the elderly. I have ministered to the aged as Hospice Chaplain for over twenty years, pastored an elderly congregation for over twenty-one years and presently serve over 650 seniors as the PACE Spiritual Care Coordinator.

Like my grandfather, I take enormous pleasure in spending quality time with aging adults. I love listening to their stories, praying with them;

rendering ministry of presence, laughing with them, comforting them in their grief, playing Bingo and cards; singing with them; worshipping with them, assisting them with their meals; preaching and teaching the Word of God, hearing their words of wisdom; taking a stroll down memory lane and embracing them with love.

Ironically, the one aging adult that I want to serve and share my love is 732.8 miles away. My dear mother, the daughter of Henry Shields lives in an assistant living residence in Atlanta Georgia. Unfortunately, the distance between Detroit and Atlanta limits my ability to see her as often as I would like. Fortunately, she lives in a beautiful place which provides all her medical, social and recreational needs. Moreover, my three sisters Dee Ann, Cherise and Renee are there for her emotional and spiritual support. My brothers David and Van live in Rochester N.Y. and fully support our mother's wellbeing from afar.

I wrote this book inspired by my Grandfathers service, my sister's compassionate caregiving and my mother's wonderful spirit. I pray this book will affirm them as they care for our virtuous mother. Also, I hope this work will inspire Pastors, Chaplains, Physicians, Administrators, C.E.O, Social Workers, Nurses, Health Aides, Recreational therapist, Geriatric workers, Hospice clinicians and caregivers to help seniors age gracefully.

Acknowledgments

I must acknowledge our Lord and Savior Jesus Christ who inspires me to serve and write about aging adults. I thank Him for giving me the opportunity and privilege to minister to seniors and the terminally ill. I received so much wisdom and knowledge from our seniors. I have thoroughly enjoyed every life story, testimony, word of encouragement and wise counsel. The elderly has taught me more about God and life than any Ivy league professor.

I praise God for my wonderful wife and children Alexandria and Samuel. I am especially proud of my wife. She is the Director of PACE Southeast Michigan Thome Rivertown location which is a program for all-inclusive care for the elderly. My wife's insights were an enormous contribution to this work. I love and appreciate her and pray that we will age gracefully together.

I thank and praise God for my siblings David, Dee Ann, Cherise, Renee and Van who have demonstrated the real meaning of *Agape* to our mother. The unconditional and unlimited love they give her is amazing. I am very grateful and proud of each of them.

I cannot praise God enough for my dear mother. She loves all her children and makes us feel special. We would not be the successful, spiritual adults we are if it had not been for our mother. Her love and laughter are what shaped and sustain us.

Personally, I am grateful for my mother's eternal love. It was her love that raised my low self-esteem as a child; challenged me to pursue higher education as a teen; affirmed my call to the ministry as a young adult; healed my broken heart in divorce; blessed my second marriage, affirmed me as a father, and inspired me as a writer. Moreover, my mother's exemplary lifestyle is one of the motivating factors to the writing of this book.

I must acknowledge all the members of Friendship Baptist Church and their support. I would be remiss if I did not acknowledge the Deacon Ministry, Rev. Greer-Stevens and the nursing home ministry, and Mrs. Maxine McBride and the Senior Support Group. They have done an amazing job of caring for the elderly.

I am grateful for the written endorsements of PACE SEMI, CEO, Mary Nabors, Dr. Gwen Graddy Chief Medical Officer of PACE SEMI, Dr. Evan Funger, Director of Operations-West Sue Hammel, RN., and Linda Bazzy, LMSW, Ms. Maxine McBride, Chairperson of Friendship Baptist Church Senior Support Group and President Ken Harris of the Ecumenical Theological Seminary. I truly appreciate their support and enormous contribution to serve humanity. A special thanks to my spiritual sister, member and editor Mrs. Elaine Rainey. Thank you again for all your ardous work.

Finally, I am eternally grateful for every Pastor, Deacon, Chaplain, Physician, Nurse, Social Worker, Health Aide, Recreational Therapist, Physical Therapist, Geriatric Worker, Dietician, Hospice clinician, Administrator, secretary, caregiver, and child of God who contributes to the health and welfare of aging adults. There is no amount of compensation that can ever equate to the countless hours, soulful sacrifice, sleepless nights, emotional exhaustion, bouts of frustration, burden of grief and silent tears you shed on behalf of the elderly. I pray that God will strengthen you for your service and one day reward you with the immortal words, *"Well done, thou good and faithful servant, thou hath been faithful over a few things. I will make you a ruler over many things. Enter into the joy of the Lord."*

Introduction

What is the secret to aging gracefully? We cannot turn back the hands of time or drink from a fountain of youth? How can we assist aging adults to enjoy their "Golden Years?" Aging is an inevitable process and it has its challenges. The immortal actress Bette Davis is right, "Old age is not for sissies." What can Pastors, Deacons, Physicians, Administrators, Clergy, Nurses, Social Workers, Health Aides, Recreational Therapist, Geriatric Workers, Hospice Clinicians, and Caregivers do to comfort and strengthen aging adults? How can we help our elderly patients, neighbors, parents, church members or loved one's age gracefully? What can we do to give them a sense of peace, love and joy?

Aging Gracefully: Spiritual Care for Aging Adults provides the spiritual knowledge and tools needed to care for seniors. It is an excellent resource for Chaplains, Pastors, Healthcare providers and caregivers as they serve the aged and the terminally ill. It provides practical information and spiritual coping skills needed to address the exigencies of aging adults. It was written for everyone who cares for seniors or wants to know how to age gracefully.

The first Chapter educates us on the *Spirituality of Aging Adults* and the differences between religion and spirituality. The better we understand the spirituality of aging adults, the better we can serve them.

The second Chapter shares the various *Spiritual Assessments* available for clergy, healthcare providers and caregivers. A Spiritual Assessment is vital to discovering the spiritual needs and concerns of aging adults. Also, caregivers must ask certain reflective questions to learn about the faith of their love one.

The third Chapter tells us how to give *Spiritual Care* to aging adults.

Logo therapy, Listening, Life Review, Learning and Love are the spiritual tools required to help them to age gracefully.

The fourth Chapter informs us on how to develop a *Spiritual Care Support Group*. The purpose of a Spiritual Care Group is to allow aging adults the opportunity to learn and express their feelings, thoughts and concerns in a non-judgmental, nurturing environment. Various discussion topics like: Carpe Diem, Stroll down Memory Lane, Hope, Peace of Mind, How to Forgive, Positive Thinking, Aging Gracefully and others will create a lively conversation and enhance their learning. The Spiritual Care Support Group can be especially useful in a PACE center, Church, Nursing Home or assisted living setting.

The fifth Chapter was written to inform and inspire aging adults to overcome the challenges of the aging process. Practicing *Spiritual Values*: Peace, Faith, Hope, Love, Joy and Grace will enhance their spiritual growth and development. These universal virtues are the secret to aging gracefully.

Finally, Chapter six was written to encourage clergy, healthcare providers and caregivers to take care of themselves. Caring for the elderly can be physically and emotionally exhausting and lead to burn out. It is critical that everyone use spiritual coping skills to ensure their spiritual and emotional health.

We are not victims of aging, sickness, and death. We can choose to age gracefully. It is up to us to choose how we will respond to the aging process. We could surrender to our pain, suffering and loss. Or we can look inward and discover the grace in our souls, love in our hearts and peace of mind.

Aging gracefully is the transformation and beautification of the soul through the acceptance and application of spiritual values.

Aging gracefully is an inside job. It is a spiritual inner transformation that empowers us to choose joy over sorrow and hope over despair. It is a positive perspective that appreciates life with all its unpredictability, vulnerabilities, and disabilities. Aging gracefully is a manifestation of the soul that is at peace with life and with God.

Betty Friedan is right, "Aging is not lost in youth but a new stage of opportunity and strength." Every day we get up in the morning is another opportunity to empower ourselves and others to age gracefully. Let us not waste time, crying, complaining and procrastinating. Let us seize the day, enjoy life, and love one another. Let us appreciate the wisdom, experience, gifts and spirituality of aging adults. Let us give them their flowers now while they can smell them and enjoy the fragrance.

CHAPTER 1

Spirituality of Aging Adults

> Grow old with me the best is yet to be.
> —Robert Browning

> Your face is marked with lines of life, put there by love and laughter, suffering and tears. It's beautiful.
> —Lynsay Sands

Many seniors age gracefully. We are male, female, black, white, yellow, and brown. We are rich, poor, middle class, working class, and underclass. We have different socioeconomic backgrounds, ethnicities, nationalities, and educational levels. We are married, single, divorced, separated, or living with a companion. We are straight, gay, and bisexual. Some of us believe in a religion, and others are agnostic, atheist, or humanist. We are Democrats, Republicans, independents, socialists, conservatives, and liberals. It does not matter what our race, class, creed, political perspective, religion, or level of morality is. *We are all spiritual beings.*

There is a depth of spirituality with aging adults. Some have learned a great deal of wisdom from life's adversities and afflictions. Despite possible physical and mental disabilities, they are independent and have developed their moral character. Others are living with their family members or reside in assisted living facilities. All of them are attempting to live on their own terms. In the words of the hip-hop artist Jill Scott, they are "living their lives like it's golden."

On the other hand, there are aging adults who appear to be wasting away physically and emotionally. They sit alone in the corridors of nursing homes with virtually no one to talk to. Some of them are in wheelchairs, and others are bedridden. Some are alert and oriented, and others are struggling with dementia. Regardless of their physical or emotional limitations, they are spiritual beings worthy of respect, love, and care.

All persons regardless of their age, gender, sexual orientation, level of consciousness, physical disabilities, socioeconomic background, level of morality, or life expectancy are spiritual. There is a spirituality in all of us that transcends man-made categories and binds us together as the human family. Soren Kierkegaard is right: "We are not human beings having a spiritual experience, we are spiritual beings having a human experience."

We are essentially spiritual beings, and we must not let ageism blind us to seeing the grace, wisdom, and beauty of the elderly and physically challenged.

The aging process has a way of revealing our spiritual identity. The older we get, the more of ourselves we lose. We lose our physical health, but we gain our spiritual wisdom and strength. The aging adults are on a spiritual journey of understanding themselves and a greater power outside themselves. Moreover, religion and spirituality appear to play a key role in the aging process and foster a better quality of life and contentment.

Many scholars have discovered that middle and later life involve an experience of increasingly transcendent aspects of inner life.[1] Achenbaum and Orwoll tied the development of wisdom to an increasingly transcendent attitude toward oneself, toward relationships with others, and toward worldly aims.[2] As age increases, many people perceive themselves as having increasingly transcendent attitudes. They take more delight in their inner worlds, are less fearful of death, and feel a greater connection to the entire universe.[3]

> *Spiritual practices help us move from identifying with the ego to identifying with the soul. Old age does that for you too, it spiritualizes people naturally.*
> *—Ram Dass*

Aging is a journey that includes a spiritual dimension that focuses on meaning in life, hope, and purpose explored through relationships with others, with the transcendent. Living longer brings with it the possibilities of enhanced health, happiness, and productivity. It is a journey home to the silence from which one came. On the way home, a nonpersonal state of consciousness may be gradually uncovered by conditions common in later life: a quiet mind, a simplified daily life, and a "let it be" attitude toward the world. The deepening spirituality of later life is often subtle and nondeliberate; it may occur naturally and spontaneously because of the physical, mental, and social processes of aging. J. M. Thibault described the conditions under which many people experience aging as a "natural monastery."[4]

Natural Monastery

There are many aging adults who experience a *natural monastery*. This is a very important concept, since the spiritual domain is one area that still provides room for growth during senior years. The body may break down, but the soul is still capable of growth, renewal, or redemption. Despite changes, losses, and chronic health conditions, aging adults can continue to cultivate the spirituality of their souls.

Many aging adults may not be religious, but they are spiritual. They do not go to church, temple, or synagogue but are still spiritual. They have their own sets of values, beliefs, and passions that enable them to live on their own terms. They are guided by their principles, intuition, feelings, and core values. Many of them are at peace with themselves, others, the world, and their God. The natural monastery is a spiritual perspective that ultimately fosters a sense of serenity, hope, love, and joy.

> ***The reason old souls enjoy spending time alone is because they never really are.***

My mother, Anna Mae White, lives alone within her own natural monastery. She is a widow aging gracefully because of her spirituality. She has a conventional faith in God but does not go to church. She does not engage in any religious rituals or practices. However, her spirituality has made her a friendly, caring person who loves life and people. She is at peace with herself and others. Her motto is "Live, laugh, and learn, and eat your dessert first."

The aging process with all its challenges has not broken her spirit or tempered her resolve to live to the fullest. She is eighty-four years old but has a childlike spirit. She has a wonderful sense of humor, and her laughter fills a room. It is her laughter and joy for life that I admire.

> ***You don't stop laughing when you grow old,***
> ***you grow old when you stop laughing.***
> ***—George Bernard Shaw***

She loves playing bingo every day and listens to every genre of music from Beethoven to B.B. King. She can socialize with many friends or sit in silence and solitude with a delightful book. My mother enjoys eating her chicken and waffles and does not mind assisting people in need.

She takes pride in the accomplishments of her adult children and lives for her great-grandchildren. Her primary purpose in life is to share her love and wisdom with her family. She uses her many picture albums as history books to reflect on our past and inspire us for the future. My mother possesses a spirituality that has made her age gracefully.

What Is Spirituality?

Spirituality is not religion, doctrines, rituals, traditions, systematic theology, or a code of morals and ethics. Spirituality is a search for meaning with or without God. It recognizes the human need for ultimate meaning in life, whether this is through relationships with God or some sense of another or whether some other sense of meaning becomes the guiding force within the individual's life.

Spirituality is multidimensional in that it encompasses every aspect and concern of an individual. Everyone and every need has a spiritual essence.

Spirituality encompasses wide-ranging attitudes and practices that focus on the meaning in human lives, particularly in terms of relationships, values, and the arts. It is concerned with quality of life, especially in areas that have not been closed off by technology and science. Spirituality may, or may not, be open to ideas of transcendence and to the possibility of the divine.[5]

Scientists who study spirituality and aging have concluded that spirituality increases with age. Many aging adults concentrate on the interior life and enhancing their relationships with God and their loved ones. In a conference on spirituality and health, they concluded that both religion and spirituality have "sacred cores" that involve "feeling, thought, experiences, and behaviors that arise from a search for the sacred."[6]

> *Just as a candle cannot burn without fire,*
> *men cannot live without a spiritual life.*
> *—Buddha*

Gerontologists explain spirituality with a definition that came from the 1971 White House conference on aging. It is the basic value around which all other values are focused, the central philosophy of life—whether religious, antireligious, or nonreligious—which guides a person's conduct, the supernatural and nonmaterial dimensions of human nature.[7] The factors that determine spirituality are:

- an understanding of self that is defined in the context of relationships to others
- an understanding of a creation story and symbols of faith
- an understanding of greater power that is outside of the self; you are intimately connected with the sense of self

Spirituality has to do with life's meaning and purpose. It is those ideas, practices, and commitments that nurture, sustain, and shape the fabric of human lives, whether as individuals or communities.[8]

> *It is a fine thing to establish one's own religion*
> *in one's heart, not to be dependent on tradition*
> *and second-hand ideals. Life will seem to you,*
> *later, not lesser, but a greater thing.*
> *—D. H. Lawrence*

Spiritual Seniors

As seniors develop spiritually, they focus on connecting with others, finding meaning and purpose in life, and holding personal power to influence outcomes. They age gracefully by changing their relationships to time; becoming more attentive, patient, and present; and often giving themselves permission to speak their truth even when it is unpopular.

There are spiritual characteristics that many elderly people possess. The following criteria reveal the identities, purposes, values, perspectives, and practices of many spiritual seniors. Gerontologist Mitroff and Denton discovered that spiritual seniors manifested the following values:

- Being inclusive, embracing everyone
- Being the ultimate source and provider of meaning and purpose in life
- Feeling awe in the presence of the transcendent
- Having inner serenity
- having an inexhaustible source of faith

Moreover, spiritual seniors take more time to reflect on the meaning of events. They feel despair over the injustices and evils in the world, long to make peace with imminent death and beliefs about death. They struggle to understand why so many good people suffer. Consequently, many seniors desire the following:

- Seek a comprehensive and more satisfying personal philosophy
- Yearn for solitude and silence
- Seek to communicate unspoken love to others
- Recognize the need for a greater sense of community
- Questions beliefs about death and the after life

RELIGIOUS SENIORS

Spirituality and religious participation are highly correlated with positive successful aging as much as diet, exercises, mental stimulation, self-efficacy and social connectedness. Religion can enable the elderly to age gracefully.

"Give me that old time religion" – Charles Davis Tillman

Religion plays a significant role in the lives of most seniors. In fact, a recent Gallup poll shows 73 percent of seniors identify religion as being very important to them. (Gallup Organization, 2002) Older adults who are more religious tend to demonstrate greater wellbeing than those who are not. [9] Elderly religious people are members of a Church. Many of them have served as ushers, choir members, Mothers board, Deacon ministry, Sunday School, evangelist or Missionary board. Religious seniors believe in the power of prayer to heal and deliver. They can be inspired by reading of scriptures, singing hymns or biblical preaching. Some of the beliefs and practices of religious seniors are:

- Belief in a God who loves and cares for them
- Belief in the sacredness of the Bible
- Belief in the power of prayer and appreciate someone praying for them
- Belief in life after death
- Belief in a divine judgement
- Belief in the *Royal Law*: Loving God and your neighbor as yourself.
- Enjoy talking about their beliefs
- Enjoy "testifying" about what God has done for them
- Enjoy listening to gospel music or biblical teaching
- Concern in the spiritual welfare of their family
- Love the Church and respect the Pastor
- They look forward to going to Church or having Church members visit them
- Enjoys helping others or "doing Gods' will"
- Their faith may struggle to accept suffering and death

Many religious people in nursing homes and assisted living residents are unable to attend their sacred institution, so they enjoyed visits from the Pastor, Deacon, chaplain or Spiritual Care Provider. Many of my visits were like mini Bible studies in which I would read their favorite passage of scripture, expound on its meaning and allow them to reflect and talk about it. All my visits were closed with prayer. It did not matter what their beliefs or religious affiliation, they wanted me to pray for God to heal and deliver them. Many of them wanted me to pray for their estranged adult children or grandchildren.

"So even to old age and gray hairs, O God, do not forsake me, until I proclaim your might to another generation, your power to all those to come." Psalm 71:18-NRSV

Religious seniors are committed to God and doing Gods will. Despite their physical challenges, and inability to go to Church, they engaged in religious practices. Some watched religious television shows or listened to gospel music on the radio. Others, are concerned about the welfare of their roommate and what they could to do to care for them. Religious seniors are mentors or surrogate mothers for health aides sharing their wisdom and grace. Many religious seniors who practice their faith are living gracefully.

There is a story about an octogenarian African American widow who was terminally ill living in a nursing home. She had a warm gentle spirit and was a charter member of a Baptist Church. She loved the Lord and did not mind sharing her faith with others. She spent most of her time in her room listening to a religious radio station and reading her Bible. I enjoyed visiting her and providing scripture readings and prayer. Her beautiful smile, peaceful spirit, and praise on her lips showed the world that she was aging gracefully.

"In old age they still produce fruit; they are always green and full of sap." Psalm 92:14- NRSV

One day, I came to visit her and discovered she was not in her room. Her bed was made up, but she was not present. There was not any sign of her. It looked as if her room had been cleaned up and cleared out. I remember thinking, "Did she get sick and go to the hospital? Did she die?" I panicked and went to the nurses' station and inquired to her whereabouts. The nurse assured me that she was in her room and would help me look for her. We looked in the bathrooms, dining room, television room and therapy room and could not find her. As we were walking down the hall we heard someone praying. I looked in the room and there she was in her wheel chair alongside the bed and holding the patients hand and praying. I stood outside the door smiling and bowing my head as she prayed. After she was done praying I said, "Hey, I was looking for you." She grinned and said, "I had to be about my Fathers' business."

The widow died a long time ago but the memory of faithful service lives on. This woman and other religious seniors have a faith that ignores illness, aches and pain and does the will of God. For many elderly persons, spirituality and participation in a religious organization gives life meaning and purpose. It helps them age gracefully.

"If religion is understanding God in the collective stories of life, then spirituality is finding God in our own narrative." – **H.L. Balcomb**

For some senior's religion and spirituality overlap. For example, there are seniors who do not go to a religious institution due to physical limitations, yet they maintain a deep, private, purposeful spiritual life. However, there are fundamental differences between religion and spirituality.

RELIGIOUS VERSES SPIRITUAL

It is important to discern whether an aging adult is religious, spiritual or both. Some religious seniors have a positive view of religion and a negative view of spirituality, believing in the benefits and blessing of being a part of a closely-knit group of believers. Other seniors have a negative view of religion and a positive view of spirituality. Their painful disappointments with a religious person or institutions have made them perceive religion as divisive, destructive and its believers close-minded, intolerant and hypocritical. Spiritual seniors perceive themselves as open-minded, tolerant, and universal. Finally, there are seniors who are religious and spiritual. They have a firm religious commitment to a religious institution and they are in touch with the passion and purpose of their soul.

Spirituality focuses on the internal dimensions of faith and religion focus on the external dimensions of faith. Religion is all about rituals and spirituality is all about relationships. A senior's relationships with family and friends impact their emotional well-being. Religion emphasizes piety, spirituality accentuates passion. A senior's feelings and drives are critical to understanding what is important for them. Religion promotes doctrine and spirituality pursues life's' meaning. Discovering one's purpose and focus in life is a major spiritual concern. Religion is based on an institution and spirituality is based on intuition and one's conscience. Spirituality requires a senior to be aware of the voice of their conscience as they struggle with their vices, virtues and sense of mortality. Religion tends to focus on individual morality concerns, spirituality is multidimensional as it addresses family, feelings, focus, finances, faults, and finite. [10]

Knowledge about the spirituality of seniors is a prerequisite for effective and responsible spiritual care.

Regardless, whether an aging adult is religious, spiritual or both they all should be revered and appreciated. We may not agree with someone's beliefs or practices, but we must respect them. Respecting their spirituality means to discover and understand their needs, beliefs, feelings, values, and purposes. To add in our understanding of a senior's spiritual needs a spiritual assessment is required.

CHAPTER 2

Spiritual Assessment of Aging Adults

"I never learn anything talking. I only learn things when I ask questions." – Lou Holtz

"The unexamined life is a life not worth living." - Aristotle

Aging gracefully requires seniors to understand and intentionally practice their religion or spirituality. Therefore, it is vital for the healthcare provider or caregiver to understand their religious or spiritual needs. There are two ways that a person can discover the spiritual needs of an aging adult: asking them a series of reflective questions or conducting a spiritual assessment. The caregivers can ask their elderly loved one's questions and discover what their religious or spiritual concerns.

Pastors, Chaplains, Deacons, Physicians, Social Workers, Nurses, Geriatric workers and Hospice clinicians can use a documented diagnostic tool to discover the concerns, values, beliefs, passions, psychosocial and spiritual exigencies of the elderly.

"The best classroom in the world is at the feet of an elderly person." – Andy Rooney

Caregivers having an informal conversation with their elderly parents, grandparents, members of a church, friends, patients or nursing home residents can discern their spiritual concerns. Even if the caregiver is a relative or knows the elderly person, they still may learn something new by asking the right questions.

CAREGIVERS ASSESSMENT OF A RELIGIOUS SENIOR

If a senior considers themselves to be religious, then certain questions can be asked which will help a caregiver understand the senior's beliefs. Ask some of these questions or other open-ended questions to get a senior to talk about their religious beliefs. You will get to know them better and receive their wisdom.

- What kind of religion do you believe in and why?
- How does your belief in God help you?
- What is your favorite scripture and why?
- Tell me about your relationship with God? How do you feel about God and why?
- Were you active in your Church and if so, what did you do and why?
- What do you miss most about going to Church?
- What is your favorite Hymn, gospel or Spiritual and why?
- What do you think God wants you to do for the rest of your life?
- How are you using your gifts, talents and experiences for God?
- Do you have difficulties or questions about your faith?
- What do you think that you need to do to prepare yourself to meet your Maker? What do you think will happen when you die?
- What do you praise God about?
- What is your testimony?
- How does your religion help you to age gracefully?
- What has God done for you?

Another method used to learn about the religious needs of an elderly person is to ask them *fill in the blank questions* which will stimulate deeper conversations about their faith.

- What I love about God is_____.
- God helps me to_____.
- God wants me to_____.
- God is pleased when I _____.
- I pray that God will_____.
- The one question I have for God is_____.
- God delivered me from_____.
- God healed me when_____.
- My greatest testimony of God is_____.

Asking religious questions or fill in the blank questions will enlighten caregivers about a senior's religious perspectives and priorities. They will discover what they think about God and how their faith comforts or even challenges them.

These questions were helpful to me as a caregiver to my late mother-in-law Mildred Clifton. She faithfully attended a Baptist Church, worked on the Usher Board, was a Sunday School teacher, and did missionary work. She was a deeply religious person who enjoyed reading the Bible, praying and listening to religious radio.

I thought I knew my Mother-in- laws religious perspective until I asked her some of these questions. I did not know how strong her faith was. Mildred believed "faith without works is dead." Therefore, she would not sit still, and was always active doing something. Despite of the fact, that she was a widow, had stomach cancer, experienced the tragic death of an adult son, and had congestive heart failure, she was very active driving to her Church, grocery shopping, and visiting her grandchildren in her eighties!!

"When I stand before God at the end of my life, I would hope that I would not have a single bit of talent left, and could say, I used everything you gave me." -Erma Bombeck

Many times, Mildred would reflect on her life and testify how the

Lord was with her as a little girl in Arkansas, and as a young adult marching and protesting segregation. She fought racism, sexism, grief, cancer, poverty, sickness, suffering and even death. She did not go *gentle into that good night*. She was a fighter even to the end of her life.

It is very important for caregivers to ask religious seniors questions about their faith and practices. It helps the caregiver to understand the elderly persons beliefs and affirms their faith. They will enjoy the opportunity to share their testimony and beliefs. Lastly, the discussion will ultimately foster an emotional and spiritual bond between the religious senior and the caregiver.

CAREGIVERS ASSESSMENT OF A SPIRITUAL SENIOR

There may be seniors who are not religious but spiritual. Some of them are atheist, agnostic, humanist or a believer in God but reject all organized religion. Some have had a bad Church experience and are angry at clergy or Church members, others attended the Church when they were younger and eventually drifted away from it. Some have never had the opportunity to bond with a religious community. Many are physically unable to go to Church and sit for extended periods of time. There are aging adults who are mentally challenged or unable to articulate their spirituality.

"I now urge friends and acquaintances to have conversations with their aging parents and within their families while their parents are still relatively healthy and of sound mind."- Lisa J. Schultz

We need to talk to our seniors. It matters not what their physical, mental or emotional challenges are, they are spiritual because of their values, beliefs, feelings passions, and or purpose in life. Caregivers can discover the spirituality of an aging adult by asking them questions or asking someone about the elderly persons spirituality.

- What is your primary purpose in life?
- What gives your life meaning?

- What is it that you enjoy doing?
- What is your passion in life?
- What or who inspires you?
- What are your hobbies?
- What did you do for a living?
- What are your goal(s)?
- What is your vision of the future?
- What are your gifts, talents or skills?
- What else do you want to do before you die?
- Are their issues or problems that you want to address?
- What is your favorite music?
- How does your spirituality help you to age gracefully?

Caregivers asking some of these questions can learn a lot about the elderly persons spirituality. If a senior is suffering from dementia, a family member or close friend can share vital information about their passions, concerns or spiritual needs.

There is a fictitious story I tell of an elderly woman with dementia living in a nursing home. Moreover, she had lost the ability to talk and walk and was bedridden. Her devoted adult daughter visited everyday but did not know how to care for her spiritually.

I asked the daughter, "What are your mothers hobbies or interests? She said, "My mother used to love gardening. She would spend countless hours tending her rose garden." I told her, "Go home take some pictures of her roses and other flowers and put them in a picture album and show them to her."

The next day the daughter brought the picture album of her rose garden and showed her mother. Her mother stared at the pictures and had a big broad smile that lit up the room. Her mother loved that picture album so much that every visit they would look at it. Looking at flowers together brought them peace and joy. The daughter had fulfilled the spiritual need of her mother.

CLINICAL SPIRITUAL CARE ASSESSMENT

A more formal, in-depth, documented Spiritual Assessment may be required from a Physician, Chaplain, Gerontologist, Social Worker, Nurse, Hospice clinician, Spiritual Care Provider, or Geriatric worker. There are many kinds of Spiritual Assessments that one can use in a hospital, nursing home or assisted living setting. Each of them has their own strengths and weaknesses. Choose a Spiritual Assessment that you feel comfortable with and best discovers their spiritual needs.

FOUR SPIRITUAL QUESTIONS

- Is faith (religion, spirituality) important to you in this illness?
- Has faith been important to you at other times in your life?
- Do you have someone to talk to about religious matters?
- Would you like to discuss religious matters with someone? [11]

Asking these four questions can help clergy, and healthcare providers understand a patients religious and spiritual beliefs. [12]

PSYCHOSOCIAL SPIRITUAL ASSESSMENT

1. Discover their Religious needs- praying for and with others, reading spiritual/religious books, and turn to a higher presence
2. Discover their Existential needs- reflect previous life, talk with someone about meaning in life/suffering, talk about the possibility of a life after death
3. Discern their need for Inner Peace- wish to dwell at places of quietness and peace, enjoying nature, talking about fears and worries, and devotion by others
4. Discern their need for giving/generativity which addresses the active autonomous intention to solace someone, to pass on life experiences to others, and be assured that life was meaningful and of value.

LIFE SATISFACTION ASSESSMENT

Life satisfaction assessment asks questions about family, friendships, where one lives, financial situation, health situation, and ability to manage one's daily life. Each of these items was introduced with the phrase "I would describe my level of satisfaction as …" and scored on a 7-point scale ranging from dissatisfaction to satisfaction (0- terrible, 1- unhappy, 2- mostly satisfied, 3 – mixed, 4- (equally satisfied and dissatisfied 5- mostly satisfied and 6 – delighted.)

QUALITY OF LIFE IN ELDERS WITH MULTIMORBIDITY

Life satisfaction assessment is used to determine the elderly persons priorities. Participants are invited to designate five domains which are important to provide meaning, satisfaction, and well-being in their life. Then each of these dimensions is scored on a 6-point scale to assess both satisfaction and relative importance.

MOOD STATES ASSESSMENT

To assess mood states which are related to life satisfaction and subjective quality of life, is based on the ASTS scale ("Aktuelle Stimmungslage") of Dalbert. It measures the state component of subjective wellbeing and differentiates four mood states, that is, positive mood, sorrow, despair, and tiredness. [13]

SPIRITUAL HISTORY ASSESSMENT

Understanding the spiritual history of seniors can be obtained by using spiritual history tools, including **FICA** (Faith, belief, meaning; Importance/influence in healthcare decision making; Community; Address/Action in treatment plan), **HOPE** (Sources of Hope ; Organized religion; Personal spirituality; Effect on medical care and end -of-life issues) and **SPIRIT** (Spiritual beliefs; Personal beliefs; Integration with spiritual community; Rituals ; Implications for care and Terminal care).

These spiritual assessments are helpful in discerning the spiritual needs of seniors. However, a more comprehensive assessment is needed to understand the spiritual, emotional, relational, emotional, financial, and moral exigencies of the elderly. The writer developed a diagnostic tool called *Multidimensional Spiritual Assessment*.

MULTIDIMENSIONAL SPIRITUAL ASSESSMENT

A *Multidimensional Spiritual Assessment* reviews an aging adults Feelings, Family, Faith, Focus, Faults, Finances and thoughts on the Finite. The Chaplain or healthcare provider can discuss these concern with seniors and discover the priority of *their* needs. This is an excellent diagnostic tool to discover the multiplicity of needs of the elderly. It can help the Chaplain or healthcare provider discover the elderly persons primary needs and concerns. [14] Also, a scale is provided to measure the patient's satisfaction with their spiritual need and the effectiveness of *Spiritual Care Plan*. Examples of a *Multidimensional Spiritual Assessment* and a *Spiritual Care Plan* can be found in the Appendices.

Feelings are a window into the soul and can indicate the healthiness of our spirituality. Grief about the death of a loved one, fear about a terminal illness, frustrations about quality of life issues, remorse over past mistakes, loneliness, sadness, depression are just some of the feelings aging adults may have. All feelings stem from our spirituality. Therefore Clergy, Physician, Social Worker, and Nurse must ask questions and understand the feelings and the spiritual issues behind the words.

Family and relationships are critical to understanding to a senior's spirituality. If a senior's relationships are important to them and they are struggling with her adult children that will impact their emotional and existential health. We must ask questions about the elderly persons family dynamics to address their spiritual needs.

Focus indicates your purpose and meaning in life. It is essential to understand what drives, motivates, inspires an elderly person. Knowing their passion will enable the Clergy and health care provider to support the seniors. The redevelopment of their purpose or vision in life is a primary concern.

Faith is what one places their ultimate trust in. Everyone has faith in someone or something. For some aging adults their faith is in God, Pastor, Church, religion, philosophy, themselves, and others. For others, their faith is reflected in their spirituality and not their religion. It is important for the Clergy or health care providers to acknowledge their faith and fortify it.

Finances and material concerns may be paramount to aging adults. Some may be concerned about the sky rocketing medical cost which fill them with worry. Others may be preoccupied with their quality of life issues: food, medical care, clothing, condition of the room etc. The Chaplain and the Social Worker can be very helpful addressing their financial or material concerns.

Faults are moral or ethical problems that plague the conscience of aging adults. Some seniors may have regrets about past mistakes or bad decisions. They feel guilty about what they have done and want to confess to someone. Some seniors may be struggling with an addiction, vice and clergy, Physician, Nurse, Therapist or Social Worker can provide counseling.

Finite or end of life issues may be a primary concern for aging adults. They may be thinking about death and dying and need someone to counsel them. Or they may need help making their final arrangements i.e. DNR papers, Burial insurance, Last Will and Testament which the Social Worker can be very helpful.

The impending death of an aging adult must be handled with a great deal of spiritual sensitivity and skill. The Physician, Chaplain, Healthcare provider and caregiver should be aware of the physical and emotional signs of the dying process. Some of these changes are gradual and some maybe a rapid downward progression. *PACE of Southeast Michigan* under the dynamic leadership of Dr. Graddy and Dr. Funger have developed an End of Life department that has published the following symptoms and signs of approaching death.

END OF LIFE CARE

SYMPTOM: Patient seems unresponsive, withdrawn, or in a comatose-like state.

RESPONSE: Speak in a normal tone, identify yourself, hold the patients hand, say whatever you need to say that will help the person "let go."

SYMPTOM: Patient claims to have spoken to persons who have already died, or to have seen places not accessible or visible to you.

RESPONSE: Do not contradict, belittle, or argue about what the patient claims to have seen or heard. Affirming their experiences will calm them.

SYMPTOM: Continually performs repetitive or restless tasks. Patient may have something that is unresolved or unfinished which prevents him/her from letting go.

RESPONSE: Work with others to help the person find release from tension and fears, give assurances that it is okay to let go.

SYMPTOM: The patient may make a seemingly out-of-character statement, gesture or request.

RESPONSE: Accept the moment when it is offered. Kiss, hug, hold, cry and say whatever you most need to say.

SYMPTOM: Patient seems to be holding on, even though it brings increased discomfort

RESPONSE: Reassure the patient, assure them that it is okay to let go.

SYMPTOM: Patient is ready to say goodbye.

RESPONSE: Stay close, hug, speak softly, say "I love you" or share happy memories. Crying is okay. These things express your love and help you to let go.

End of Life Care is critical to the spiritual welfare of patient and caregiver. Often the terminally ill patient has already made peace with the fact that they are dying, and caregiver and their families struggle to accept it. It is essential that the Chaplain, Spiritual Care Provider, Pastor, Deacon, Physician, Nurse, Health Aide, Social Worker, and caregiver be willing to do the following:

- Render ministry of presence. Spend quality time with family and encourage them to share their feelings and thoughts. Empathize with them.
- *Offer* prayer (They may refuse)
- Encourage family to verbalize their love to their dying loved one

- Encourage family to gather around the patient's bedside, hold hands and pray for peaceful transition
- *Offer* individual counseling to family, especially to children and teens
- Discourage any arguing or intense discussions around the dying
- Encourage family members to share positive thoughts about the dying
- Encourage family members to take care of themselves. Get rest, eat well, pray and not burn themselves out.
- *Offer* to read comforting scriptures
- *Offer* to contact their clergy or make referral to Chaplain or Spiritual Care Provider

"Do not cast me off in the time of old age; Do not forsake me when my strength is spent."- Psalm 71:9-NRSV

Multi-Dimensional Spiritual Assessment covers a wide range of issues and concerns which may overlap with the Social Workers Assessment. For example, the financial concerns are dealt with by the Social Worker, however it becomes a Chaplains issue when the senior is full of worry and anxiety. The following is an example of *Multi-Dimensional Assessment*.

MULTIDIMENSIONAL SPIRITUAL ASSESSMENT

1. ***FEELING***

    How do you feel most of the time? (Circle all that apply)
    Happy, Sad, Angry, Frustrated, Hopeful, Bored, Worried, Anxious, Fearful, Content, Peaceful, Weak, Tired, Hopeless, Depressed, Joyful, Agitated, Hopeless, Helpless, Bitter, Guilty, Cynical, Pessimistic, Doubtful, Inspired, Remorseful, Energized, Lonely, Respected, Other

    _____

    Why do you feel this way?
    _____
    _____

What or who gives you a sense of joy?
_____
_____

In what ways do you feel loved and appreciated?
_____
_____

What or who gives you peace of mind?
_____
_____

What or who upsets you?
_____
_____

2. **FAMILY**

   How would you characterize your relationship with your primary caregiver and or family? (Circle all that apply) Peaceable, Strained, Dysfunctional. Loving, Nurturing, Disconnected, Disrespectful, Competitive, Proud, Argumentative, Lack of Trust, Angry, Hostile, Domineering, Submissive, Abusive, Respectful, Caring, Sad, Supportive, Empowering, Joyful, Contentious, Content, needs improvement, Rejected, Abandoned,
   Are there any relationships that you want to work on?
   _____
   _____

   In what ways do you feel loved or unloved by your family
   _____
   _____

3. **FOCUS**

   What is your focus or purpose in life. What gives your life meaning?
   _____
   _____

   What is your hobby or what do you love to do?
   _____
   _____

   What is your vision or what do you want to accomplish in life?
   _____
   _____

What or who gives you a sense of hope?
_____
_____

4. **FAITH**

   What or who do you place your ultimate faith in?
   _____

   Are your religious, spiritual or both?
   _____

   How does your religion or spirituality help you?
   _____

   What questions or faith challenges do you have?
   _____
   _____

   What can you do to develop your faith?
   _____
   _____

   What or who inspires you? What are you passionate about?
   _____
   _____

5. **FINANCES**

   What are your financial or material concerns? (Circle all that apply) Meals, Shelter, Clothing, Living Conditions, Living Expenses, Poverty, Job, Medical Expenses, Funeral Arrangements, Life Insurance, Last Will & Testament, Indebtedness, Family Expenses, Transportation, Social Security, Retirement plans, Other

6. **FAULTS**

   Do you have any faults, weaknesses that you are concerned with? (Circle all that apply) Substance Abuse, Gluttony, Need to Exercise, Gambling, Sexual Promiscuity, Hoarding, Toxic Guilt, Constantly worry, lack of spirituality, lack of morality, lack of faith, lack of a meaningful life, hopelessness, procrastination, Apathy, Alcoholism, addiction, Anger, Bad temper, negative attitude, other

_____
_____
_____
_____
_____
_____

7. **FINITE**

   How do you feel about dying? (Circle all that apply)
   Sad, Angry, Afraid, Troubled, Depressed, Happy, Fearful, Peaceful, Struggling to Accept, Denial, Hopeful, Helpless, do not want to talk about it, Do not think about it, Accepting, Upset, Anxious, Worried,
   What do you need to do to prepare yourself for death? (Circle all that apply) Receive Spiritual Counseling, Develop a Last Will and Testament, Make Funeral Arrangements, Talk to my family, Talk to Pastor or clergy, Check insurance and burial papers, read literature on death and dying, deal with anticipatory grief issues, Look at DNR paperwork, Review Medical Power of Attorney Papers, Other [15]

A Spiritual Assessment is necessary to discover the spiritual needs of aging adults. A caregiver can ask their alert loved ones about their religion or spirituality and affirm their faith. Physicians, Chaplains, Social Workers, Nurses and healthcare providers can use one of the diagnostic tools mentioned above, however a *Multidimensional Spiritual Assessment* will be extremely helpful for clinicians. They will learn about the many needs or concerns of seniors, so that they can provide good spiritual care.

SPIRITUAL CARE NEEDS OF AGING ADULTS

The aging adults have universal spiritual needs. A compilation of statistical research from over 1200 empirical studies and 400 reviews by

Koenig and colleagues (1994, 2001) has revealed a connection between faith and religious practice and health benefits, including protection from illness, coping with illness and faster recovery. Koenig (1994) identified fourteen spiritual needs of older people based on prior research both at a theoretical and empirical level, Koenig here is specifically talking about religion and the various practices that emerge from participation in religion. The list below reveals some of the spiritual care needs of aging adults.

- Need for support in dealing with loss
- Need to transcend circumstances
- Need to be forgiven and to forgive
- Need to find meaning and purpose
- Need to love and serve other
- Need for unconditional love
- Need to feel that God is on their side
- Need to be thankful
- Need to prepare for death and dying
- Need for continuity
- Need for validation and support of religious behaviors
- Need for personal dignity and sense of worthiness
- Need to express anger and doubt [16]

A Physician, Nurse or Social Worker can make a referral to the Chaplain or Spiritual Care Provider based on these needs and they can follow up with Spiritual Care. An example of a PACE referral to Spiritual Care Provider is found in the Appendix.

These are only a few of the spiritual care needs of the elderly. We would be remiss to suggest that these are *all* their needs, because everyone is different. Every aging adult has their own unique history, socio-economic background, family dynamics, beliefs and values. Therefore, we must be careful about putting seniors in simplistic categories and not respecting their individuality. However, the spiritual assessments and the spiritual care needs list will educate the Clergy, healthcare provider and caregiver in the many spiritual needs of seniors and prepare them to render effective spiritual care.

CHAPTER 3

Spiritual Care for Aging Adults

"Love, care and treasure the elderly people in the society." – **Lailah Akita**

"To care for those who once cared for us is one of the highest honors."- **Tia Walker**

Spiritual care for aging adults should be motivated by compassion, person-centered, and recognize the dignity and unique spirituality of the individual. Compassion, empathy, patience and respect must rule the heart of those who are caring for the elderly. Serving them out of a sense of duty, religious obligation or for a paycheck is not good enough. One must genuinely care about those they serve. Caring not only impacts the receiver but also the giver. Harold Kushner is right, "Caring about others, running the risk of feeling, and leaving an impact on people, brings happiness."

"One person caring about another represents life's greatest value."- Jim Rohn

Spiritual care must be 'person-centered care' affirming the dignity and the diversity in everyone's spirituality. Person-centered care is currently the preferred method of providing care 'that is responsive to individual preferences, needs and values and assuring that patient values guide all clinical decisions.' [17] Every elderly person has their own spirituality and we must respect it. The last thing any Clergy person, healthcare provider or caregiver should do is superimpose their religion or spirituality on someone. The task of the Spiritual Care Provider is to assist the elderly in the exploration and understanding and development of *their* faith or spirituality. This means the Clergy person, health care provider or the caregiver must discipline themselves and not allow their religion or beliefs to prejudice their thinking or compromise their ability to serve. Spiritual care is totally person centered and makes no assumptions about the personal convictions of the elderly.

Spiritual care is a one-on-one relationship that is completely person centered and not necessarily religious care. Religious care should always be spiritual care dealing with the multiplicity of elderly needs. Therefore, spiritual Care can be rendered by Clergy, Physicians, Nurses, Social Workers, Health Aides, Recreational Activity workers, Geriatric workers, Hospice clinicians, Church workers and caregivers. Everyone can render spiritual care because everyone has a spirituality which binds all human beings together.

Spiritual care is person-centered, compassionate care that addresses a multiplicity of needs.

There are many different spiritual care tools that persons can use as they care for aging adults. Richard Lewis work *Aging as A Spiritual Practice* delineates six practices for aging well:

SPIRITUAL TOOLS

Gratitude. We should encourage a spirit of gratitude by asking the elderly what they are grateful for. Many will say they are grateful for their grandchildren, good health, free time, wearing what they want, the chance to travel, and giving back to the community. Ask your seniors to participate in a "thank you prayer" where they repeat the words "thank you" and share what they are thankful for.

Generosity. It is scientifically proven that giving back and helping others makes us feel happier and more content. Giving is a universal spiritual value taught by religion, and the desire to give back naturally increases as we age. We can encourage the elderly to find creative ways that they can serve humanity. They may not be able to do what they used to do, but they can do something. Giving and serving will help them feel wanted and give meaning to their lives.

Reframing. Aging includes its share of reverses, losses and sorrows. What makes the difference is our attitude about them. If a bad knee means we cannot jog anymore, we need not despair; we can take up swimming. If we lost money in the recession, we can cherish what we still have. If we become ill, we rejoice when we recover. The Clergy person, Healthcare provider or caregiver can help the elderly reframe their negative circumstances and change into positive one.

Curiosity. Curiosity is an important attitude to cultivate as we age. There is a tendency to hunker down in our old familiar routines, it is good to resist that temptation. Physical exercise grows new muscle, mental activity grows new brain cells, emotional engagement lifts the spirit. Curiosity keeps us young; we need to cherish it. Clergy, Physician, Nurse, Social Worker, Recreational therapist and caregiver can gently challenge seniors to learn something new.

Flexibility. Things change as we age, and some of those changes are irrevocable. Our youthful stamina is gone forever; a dying friend will never return. In the face of these changes, it is important that we not become rigid and stuck in our ways. With every reversal comes a new opportunity. No matter what the issue, no matter how big the problems, there is always something constructive that you can do. Never give up, never let aging get the better of you. Clergy, Social Worker or caregivers can share the spiritual virtues of peace, faith, hope, love, grace and joy which are listed in the last chapter, to encourage the elderly to "not go gentle into that good night."

Spiritual Life. A spiritual perspective on aging is not just for personal transformation; it is medicine for longevity and health. Research shows that people with an active involvement in church or spiritual community live on average seven years longer than those who do not. The Spiritual Care Provider, Social Worker, Nurse and

Physician can tell the elderly the physical and emotional benefits of having or developing their spiritual life. [18]

The Clergy, Physician, layperson, Social Worker, Nurse, Geriatric Worker, Hospice Clinician or caregiver can use Spiritual reminiscence, Spiritual history, Life review, Music, Worship, Presence, and Listening to help seniors to age gracefully. Each of these spiritual tools will develop their faith and spirituality.

SPIRITUAL REMINISCENCE

Discussing the past religious and spiritual events gives the Chaplain, Healthcare providers and seniors an opportunity to review spiritual needs and develop new friendships with and knowledge of each other. Life story work with an emphasis on spirituality develops stronger relationships between staff and residents and allows for discussions about meaning to take place. This is especially effective amongst dementia patients. [19]

SPIRITUAL HISTORY

Spiritual history taking involves asking about the importance of faith and beliefs of the person. We must ask the aging adult about the importance of faith, their community and what their faith compels them to do. Affirming the elderly persons spiritual history is vital to affirming their faith and wellbeing. [20]

GUIDED AUTUBIOGRAPHICAL GROUP

Birren and Schroots (2006) researched the value of life review and set up the Guided Autobiographical Group (GAB). His findings showed that GAB provided increased sense of personal power and importance and enhanced adaptive capacities, drawing on forgotten or dormant skills. This allowed people to face end of life matters with confidence. The TSAO foundation for successful aging in Singapore suggested that there are three stages to GAB:

- A general group discussion around a specific theme to trigger the process of self-awareness and life review
- Small work group that discusses a specific theme at a deeper level
- Individual work, either in writing or by audio recording on a specific theme [21]

MUSIC / SONG

The positive effects of music and singing on wellbeing are noted in Lipe's (2002) review. Robertson-Gillam (2008) carried out a pilot study to test the potential for choir work to reduce depression and increase quality of life in people with dementia, and to look at the extent to which it met their spiritual needs. Twenty-nine participants were assigned to one of three groups: choir, reminiscence and control. Results indicated increased levels of motivation and engagement. Learning the lyrics evoked long-term memory with religious and spiritual meanings for choir members. Both the choir and the reminiscence group showed improved levels of purpose and wellbeing. [22]

WORSHIP / PRAYER / RITUAL

Providing continuity for the elderly in terms of their familiar rituals and routines sustains memory and wellbeing. Atchley's (2009) longitudinal study of 1300 people over twenty years from 1975 showed that continuity of activities occurred most commonly for reading, being with friends, being with family, attending church and gardening. Goldsmith (2004) identifies the importance of continuity of worship and using familiar signs and symbols, as well as the capacity to create forms of worship that tap into spiritual memory. [23]

BEING THERE

The reflective self as a presence for others helps the spiritual journeys of others. Kelly (2012) discusses the use of the person themselves as the resource by which spiritual care can be delivered. This follows on from Speck's (1988) work which shows that the calm and unpressured presence of the chaplain can provide support in times of difficulty and when in search for meaning. [24]

LISTENING

Careful listening is a spiritual practice. Recent research into community chaplaincy listening (Mowat et al. 2012) shows that intentionally listening to another, the gift of time and attention offered, gives a sense of hope, meaning and purpose. [25]

SPIRITUAL CARE INTERVENTIONS FOR AGING ADULTS

Spiritual care interventions are necessary for seniors to age gracefully. Each intervention addresses a unique spiritual concern and fulfills the needs of the soul. Moreover, they bring healing to a broken heart, peace to a troubled mind and fulfillment to an empty soul.

"Take care of the elderly people." – Lailah Gifty Akita

Chaplains, Pastors, Deacons, Physicians, Laypersons, Social Workers, Geriatric workers, Nurses, Health Aides, Hospice clinicians and caregivers can use the following spiritual care interventions: LOVE, LISTEN, LEARNING, LIFE REVIEW, and LOGOTHERAPY. These spiritual interventions do not require any formal education. However, they do require that we deny our own religion, beliefs, and values to understand and affirm the religion or spirituality of the aged. [26]

LOVE

One of the most effective spiritual care interventions one can give to aging adults is love. There is nothing more therapeutic, liberating, nurturing, strengthening, and comforting than love. Love can do more for us than all the medicine, physicians, or therapist combined. Love is medicine for the soul and healing for a wounded spirit. There is nothing more important than giving and receiving love.

Greek philosophers had four definitions of love. *Eros* was romantic love between a man and a woman. *Philia* is friendship love. It is love that one has for friends based on mutual interest and concerns. *Storgis* is love one has for their family. It is relationship based on blood relatives. Finally, there is *Agape* which is the love of God working in the human heart. Agape is unconditional, it is for everyone regardless of their religion, race, class, gender, or level of morality. Agape is unlimited in that it places no limits on the amount of love. It is an unconquerable love, that overcomes hatred, indifference and ignorance. Paul the Apostle delineates the characteristics of Agape in the I. Corinthians 13

"If I speak in the tongues of mortals and of angels, but do not have love, I am a noisy gong or a clanging cymbal. And if I have prophetic powers and understand all mysteries and all knowledge, and if I have all faith, so as to remove mountains, but do not have love, I am nothing. If I give away all my possessions, and if I hand over my body so that I may boast, but don't have love, I gain nothing. Love is patient; love is kind, love is not envious or boastful or arrogant or rude. It does not insist on its own way; it is not irritable or resentful, it does not rejoice in wrong doing, but rejoices in the truth. It bears all things, believes all things, hopes all things, endures all things. Love never ends. But as for prophecies, they will come to an end, as for tongues they will cease, as for knowledge, it will come to an end. For we know only in part, we prophecy in part; but when the complete comes the partial will come to an end. When I was a child, I spoke as a child, I thought as a child, I reasoned as a child, when I became a man, I put away childish things. For now, we see in a mirror, dimly, but when we will see face to face. Now I know only in part; then I will know fully, even as I have been fully known. And now faith, hope, and love abide, these three; and the greatest of these is love." (I. Corinthians 13:1-13,-NRSV)

Agape is essential to providing effective spiritual care. The Clergy, healthcare providers and caregiver's primary motivation in serving seniors is love. Moreover, if Clergy, and healthcare providers do not possess compassion for the elderly they are doing themselves and those they serve a great disservice.

We do not have to feel loving to be loving.

Again, this love is not a feeling or an emotion. It is "to will the good of another", states Thomas Aquinas. We do not have to feel loving to be loving. One can show love to someone they do not like or give love to someone who is incapable of returning love. The purpose of love is to love and not seek anything in return. Love is an act of the will that can manifest itself in many simple ways. Here are just a few of the ways that the Clergy, Physician, Healthcare provider, Nurse, Geriatric worker, Social Worker, Health aide and caregiver can manifest love.

- Tell them that you love them.
- Give them a hug
- Complement them on their appearance, family members, life story etc.
- Respect their beliefs and religion even when it contrary from your own
- Listen to them even when they do not make any sense
- Smile with them
- Laugh with them
- Cry with them
- Respect them by calling them by what *they* want to be called
- Look men in the eye and give a firm handshake as a sign of respect
- Do not be preoccupied with your thoughts, focus on them
- For better understanding, repeat what *they* said to you
- Render ministry of presence, sit with them
- Hold their hand
- Offer to pray for them or with them
- Assist them as they eat their meal
- Offer them water
- Watch television with them
- Listen to music or radio with them
- Attend worship service with them
- Encourage them to "tell their life story."
- Encourage them to do their hobby or find a new one
- Clean and polish their nails
- Help them play bingo
- Ignoring insults, unjust criticism, and unreasonable behavior
- Speaking tenderly and respectfully to them

- Always treat them with respect and dignity
- Being willing to forgive the unforgivable and tolerate the intolerable

It is the seemingly insignificant things that we do for others that count. One small gesture or act of kindness can make a significant impact on a person's life. It can transform a negative attitude into a positive one and give them a whole new outlook on life. Sharing your love to aging adults can be medicine to their weary soul, putting them in a good mood. Telling a senior that you love them or giving them a hug can heal their broken heart and lift their spirits. Talking to them with respect can affirm their dignity.

I have watched heroic health aides go above and beyond the call of duty serving the elderly. Many of them expressed their compassion in giving hugs, sharing a laugh, listening to their complaints, polishing nails, enduring insults, giving them their favorite food, beautifying them and being unbelievably patient and kind.

There is a story I tell of a young African American pregnant woman who was a home health aide to a prejudiced, belligerent, angry sixty-seven-year-old white male suffering from dementia who constantly used racial insults. He had the audacity to refer to her as a "fat Black bi**." Her supervisor affirmed her and offered to send her to serve someone else. Unbelievably she insisted on going back to serve this man saying, "I don't take his words personally. I know who I am. I forgive him. Besides I have a job to do and no one and nothing can stop me from doing what I have to do." Her sense of commitment to serve despite insults and indignities demonstrates the best of Agape. We may never have to endure what this health aide had to endure, but we must be willing to go the extra mile in service to the aged. We must return evil with good and hate with love.

Loving seniors means rendering ministry of presence. There are times when the best thing a person can do is hold someone's hand and sit in silence. The ministry of presence is a way of "being" rather than "doing" or "telling." We should not think about what to say or do. We should not anticipate how to react if certain situations arise. Instead, we should inwardly prepare ourselves to focus on the "now" with feeling and care. [27] Here is what Henri Nouwen wrote about ministry of presence.

"More and more, the desire in me simply to walk around, greet people, enter their homes, sit on their door steps, play ball, throw water, and be known as someone who wants to live with them. It is a privilege to have the time to practice this simple ministry of presence. The first thing is to know people by name, to eat and drink with them, to listen to their stories and tell your own, and to let them know with words, handshakes, and hugs that you do not simply like them, but you truly love them."

The ministry of presence means that we will serve aging adults even when it might make us uncomfortable. We will stand with them during anxiety, fear, weakness, doubt, sadness and despair. Most importantly, in these tough times we will be realistic. We will not pretend things are better or worse than they are. We will be emotionally present and empathize with them. We will "weep with those who weep and rejoice with those who rejoice."

We must look beyond the diseased, disfigured, and deteriorating body and address the exigencies of the soul.

Ministry of presence means being sensitive and understanding to seniors suffering from dementia. There is a fictitious story I share about a devoted woman who lovingly cared for her mother who had dementia. Often, she would use a lot of profanity when addressing her daughter and others. The daughter would ignore it and continue to care for her. It did not matter what she said to her, she showed her love and kindness. I asked her, "How are you able to care for your mother when she continues to vilify you?" She told me, "I ignore it and remember that my mother is a loving, caring, spiritual woman of God. It is not her cursing, it's the disease." We must look beyond the deteriorating body, listen beyond the foul language and care for the soul of those suffering from dementia.

Loving seniors means giving them music therapy. Music can be medicine for the soul. It has universal appeal and can reach us on a very deep emotional and spiritual level. It can inspire joy and eradicate all our worries or bring a sense of sorrow reminding us of a painful past. Music can motivate us to do good or evil. It can encourage people to be rebellious, promiscuous and hostile or it can inspire holiness, philanthropy and community service. Music can challenge us to stand up for our rights and freedoms. Or it can fill our minds with superfluous, non-essential information that makes us happy but dulls our social consciousness. Music can motivate us to worship God and live a godly lifestyle. On the other hand, music can instill vacuous values that promote immorality, hedonism and narcissism. Some lyrics liberate the heart, mind and soul while other lyrics enslave us to the whim and caprices of the flesh. [28]

The reason why music has such an influence on the human spirit is because of its spirituality. Country western, Gospel, Spirituals, Classical, R & B, Hip-Hop, Blues, Rock & Roll, Techno-Beat and Rap is spiritual because it stems from the passions, values, ideas, frustrations, joy, sorrows, dreams and blues of people. [29]

Many seniors love music, all kinds of music. I have watched seniors become peaceful and reflective as they listened to Classical music and jazz. I have witnessed elderly persons dancing to James Brown and singing with Stevie Wonder. If we want to bring spiritual healing to aging adults and change their mood, we must give them music therapy.

I was sitting with one of my elderly patients in the recreational room of an assisted living residence. There were about twenty to twenty-five seniors in wheel chairs and jurey chairs sitting with us. Some of them appeared to be alert and others appeared lifeless, empty, sad and depressed. The atmosphere of the room was dark and dreary.

Suddenly, a dynamic recreational therapist came in the room and began to engage all the seniors saying, "Are you ready to party?!" This young, effervescent, African American woman played fifties music and transformed the entire spirit of the room. The residents were smiling, laughing and singing with the Temptations, Diana Ross and the Supremes, Four Tops, Rolling Stones, Chuck Berry, Little Richard and many others. However, the song that got some of them on their feet and dancing in their wheelchairs was *The Twist* by Chubby Checker. Some were twisting in their wheelchairs or with their walkers. Others were tapping their feet, nodding their heads or clapping their hands. They really enjoyed themselves twisting, singing and shouting. If we want to help our seniors to age gracefully we must give them music therapy.

LISTENING

"The first duty of love is to listen," says Paul Tillich. Listening is a very valuable spiritual intervention. We must endeavor to listen to the feelings, beliefs, passions, and concerns of seniors. Listening means having a non-judgmental, non-critical approach to those who are complaining, criticizing, whispering, cursing and babbling incoherently or even shouting at you. Listening does not mean that we accept or affirm everything that is said to us. It does mean that we respect the seniors right to express his or her feelings and opinions in his or her own way. Listening means entering the world of the participant and nurturing him or her. It takes good listening skills to assist aging adults and discern their needs. Dianne Schilling writer, graphic artist, educational trainer and counselor shares the following listening skills:

- Face the speaker and maintain eye contact
- Be attentive, but relaxed
- Listen to the words and try to picture what the speaker is saying
- Don't interrupt and don't impose your solutions
- Keep an open mind
- Wait for the speaker to pause to ask clarifying questions
- Ask questions only to ensure understanding
- Try to feel what the speaker is feeling
- Give the speaker regular feedback
- Pay attention to what *isn't* said- to nonverbal cues.
- Summarize what was said to you [30]

Listening skills are especially important when dealing with seniors with dementia who require more patience and understanding. There is a story I tell about the art of listening. There was an elderly Mexican American man who had dementia. I saw him walking down the hallway headed for the front door. He had his winter coat on and was carrying a suitcase. He was slowly walking down the hallway.

I asked him, "Where are you going?"

He said, "I'm going home, and this is not my home."

I warned him, "But its freezing outside and there is at least a foot of snow."

He gently pushed me aside and said, "Please get out of my way, I'm going to be late. I got to catch a train."

So, I moved aside, but I admit I was concerned. I was afraid he would walk outside of the assisted living residence and get lost somewhere. I continued to walk with him, trying to convince him to turn around and go back to his room. He got to the reception desk and asked the receptionist, "Did the train to Mexico get here yet?"

The receptionist smiled and said, "Oh no, you just missed it, but if you want to you can sit down and come back tomorrow."

I asked the receptionist what it was all about. She told me that this precious old man comes to her desk every day and ask if the train arrived to take him to Mexico. Furthermore, she pretended right along with him and acted as if he were at a train station. The receptionist never questioned him or criticized him. She entered his world and supported him. The nursing home receptionist reminded me of what it is to really listen. *Listening means entering that person's world and nurturing him or her.* [31]

LIFE REVIEW

Life Review Therapy or *Reminiscence Therapy*, is a treatment where the review of one's life gently helps alleviate depression as they enter their end stage of life. Through positive memories, current negative thoughts may be dispersed and acceptance and worth of their lifetime achievements can be appreciated. Life Review Therapy is recommended for older adults who suffer from depression, dementia, Alzheimer's disease, or who are in Hospice or end-of-life care facilities. [32]

The Spiritual Care Provider, Pastor, Chaplain, Deacon, Physician, layperson, Social Worker, Geriatric Workers, Hospice clinicians and caregivers can encourage seniors to review their life and tell their story. Many seniors want to share their rich experiences, struggles, accomplishments, regrets, victories and defeats. Life review enables the elderly to take pride in their achievements and learn from their mistakes. Reviewing their life will ultimately validate their feelings, thoughts, and beliefs. Every aging adult has a story to tell and a legacy to leave. Some elderly persons are eager to share their stories of the good "old days" and how they overcame their hardships.

Researchers are now finding that these stories of strength, character and endurance, joys, sorrows, and recovery are helping some senior citizens rebound from depression that has settled in during their elderly years or while they are nearing the end of their life. By sharing their life stories, they can look back over their years and see worth and meaning and can pass this history on to others so that a part of them will always live on. [33] Moreover, the more seniors tell their stories and share their experiences the more positive their mood will become.

The following questions or activities can be used to stimulate Life Review:

- When you look back over your life, what are you most proud of?
- What was it like growing up in the 40s', 50s' or 60s'?
- If you could go back in time, what age would you be and why?
- Share a story of how you had to overcome an adversity or loss? (death, divorce, physical illness, abuse, poverty etc.)
- What deceased person do you think about and why? What do you most miss about this person?
- Tell me about the days when you were in High School or College?
- If you could go back in time what would you change and why?
- Tell me about the time when you first met your spouse?
- What kind of parent were you?
- What kind of son or daughter were you?
- Get out a picture album and reflect on the pictures
- What kind of mother did you have? What do you most remember about her?
- What kind of father did you have and what do you most remember about him?
- Tell me something about your past
- When you look back over your life, what are you most grateful for?
- Tell me something about your family?
- Who had the most influence in your life?

- Listen to old songs to stimulate memories
- Placing old nostalgic objects in their hands to bring back memories
- If they have trouble recalling stories, help them to tell their story
- What was the happiest time of your life?
- Show them pictures of cars in the 50s', 60s', 70s' and discuss them
- Watch an old movie together and talk about it
- Look at pictures and newspaper clippings
- Recalling pleasant memories and persons in their past life

As a Pastor, I had the privilege to hear the life stories of many seniors. I will never forget a World War II veteran who was a paralyzed from the neck down. He could not move his limbs or his neck. He was a prisoner of his own body. However, his spirit soared like a free bird when he began to talk about his life. He asked me to place his pictures on his wall so that he could see them. He had pictures of his wife and fellow soldiers. After I put them on the wall, we spent hours talking about them. He enjoyed talking about his military service. His eyes lit up when he reminisced about his deceased wife. He blushed when he talked about the time when he first met her. He laughed out loud when he remembered some of his blunders. His whole demeanor changed when he reflected on his life. Life review was like medicine to his soul. [34]

LEARNING

Clergy, Deacon, Lay person, Physicians, Social Worker, Geriatric Worker and caregiver are teachers who use education as a spiritual tool for seniors. It does not matter how old a person is, where they went to school, what degrees they earned or how wise they are, they can always learn something. "There is no end to education. It is not that you read a book, pass an examination, and finish with education. The whole of life, from the moment you are born to the moment you die, is a process of learning" states, Jiddu Krishnamurti. Learning is the beginning of spirituality. Searching and learning is where the healing process begins. We are made whole when we learn who we are, and whose we are.

"A good teacher can inspire hope, ignite imagination, and instill a love of learning." – Brad Henry

Therefore, we may have to teach or reinforce the senior about their religion or enhance their spirituality. A word of wisdom, grief information, scripture reading, religious literature, bereavement information, meditation, funeral arrangement information, and medical education about their physical condition, may be what the elderly person needs to give them faith, peace, hope and joy. The right spiritual insight and information can mend a broken heart, heal a wounded spirit, open a closed mind and liberate an enslaved soul. Never underestimate the power of the spoken word.

As a hospice chaplain, I had to serve many Jehovah Witnesses who initially did not want a chaplain to visit them. Their faith prohibits them from learning from anyone other than the Jehovah Witness elders, however, I still felt a moral obligation to offer spiritual support.

The first thing that I share is that I am not there to proselytize, debate the scriptures or attempt to change their faith. I inform them that I am there to give them spiritual support and enhance their beliefs. I supported them by listening to their beliefs and reading their *Watch Tower* to them when they are physically incapacitated. This kind of unconditional support enables them to make a peaceful transition.

Spiritual support means to enhance and or educate a person's religious or spiritual perspective.

There is a story about a senior whose soul was anxious, and troubled because he did not understand why he was still dying. He had been hoping and praying to get better, but he had gotten worse. Consequently, he cried and complained to anyone who would listen.

Fortunately, the nurse was listening and gave him the medical information he needed about his illness. Also, his chaplain gave him information that would increase his faith to cope with illness. The medical and spiritual knowledge this man received was critical to his spiritual/emotional wellbeing. He had peace of mind because he was taught by his nurse and Chaplain.

There may be an aging adult whose basic faith is incapable of dealing the challenges of suffering, sickness, loss, and the dying process. The onslaught of life's troubles has shattered their faith and made them doubt themselves and God. The spiritual care provider or caregiver can read comforting scriptures or religious literature to buttress their faith. The more they learn about God and their faith, the stronger they will become.

Some seniors and their family may be grieving the death of a loved one and need information about the grieving process. Moreover, they may desire information on preparing for the end of their life. Clergy, and Social Workers can provide essential information about anticipatory grief issues, funeral preparation, Last Will and Testament, D.N.R, writing an obituary, and the grieving process. Many seniors will deeply appreciate this vital information as they prepare themselves and their families for their demise.

GRIEF COUNSELING

A Spiritual Care Provider, Pastor, Deacon, Layperson, Chaplain, or Social Worker maybe called upon to offer grief support to the families and friends of a deceased senior. Grief is a natural physical, emotional and spiritual reaction to significant loss or change. Grieving is the process of spiritual, emotional, and life adjustment one goes through after death or loss. Grief is not an illness; grief is not easy; grief is work.

The bereaved family may need to be taught about the grieving process which is "the way we express our grief which is different for everyone. There is no normal or expected period for grieving." [35] However, there is bereavement process called, *The Healing Cycle* which has three phases, Crying, Coping and Creating which fosters inner peace and comfort. [36] A Clergy person, Social Worker or caregiver can use *The Healing Cycle* for individual or Grief Support Group counseling.

THE HEALING CYCLE

CRYING

In this phase the bereaved are encouraged to express and embrace their grief. The more the bereaved embrace their loss and verbalize it the stronger they will become. Healing comes with tears, crying, complaining, mourning and grieving. The bereaved are encouraged to identify their symptoms of grief:

- Confusion, forgetfulness
- Sadness, Sobbing, Crying
- Anger, Bitterness
- Guilt, Self-reproach
- Depression
- Anxiety, Worry
- Loneliness, withdraw from others, and activities
- Despair, giving up
- Helplessness
- Shock
- Bargaining
- Fear
- Yearning
- Hypersensitivity
- Exhaustion
- Pessimism
- Weight loss
- Tearful Spells
- Confusion about the future
- Indifference
- Bland expression
- Avoidance of talking about the death of deceased or sharing feelings
- Questioning your faith and belief system
- Questioning the Meaning and Purpose of Life
- Slowed thinking and actions

Identifying the symptoms of grief and sharing them is all a part of the healing process. Grief is not something to fix or get rid of, it is a process of self-discovery, something to experience. [37]

COPING

During this phase the bereaved are still encouraged to express their grief. However, they must develop spiritual coping skills to handle their grief. The Chaplain or Social Worker can teach them how to take care of themselves spiritually, emotionally and physically. Here are some suggestions:

- Pamper yourself with hot baths, massage, eating your favorite food, listening to your favorite music, going to the Movies, etc.
- Talk to a close friend, therapist or clergy person
- Be patient with yourself and express yourself. Healing process takes time
- Healing can be a "roller coaster ride" of highs and lows.
- Healing means to learn to live with the loss.
- Healing means remembering with less pain
- Eat healthy meals or nutritional drinks until you build up your appetite
- Exercise or go for a vigorous walk to ensure your health and sleep
- Write notes to yourself or talk to a friend if you are forgetful or confused
- Do not make emotionally charged decisions that you will regret later
- Don't keep up appearances that can be stressful. Be yourself if you feel like crying, cry. If you don't want to be bothered with people, tell them
- Take time to remember your deceased loved one. Remembering and reflecting about the past brings healing and comfort.

The Chaplain, Pastor or Social Worker can discuss these spiritual care coping mechanisms to help the bereaved to function with their grief.

CREATING

The last phase of the grieving process is creating. At this session the Clergy person, Social Worker or caregiver will counsel the bereaved to create a new life for themselves which reflect their spiritual emotional growth. The facilitator will remind the bereaved of their freedom to choose the life that they want. As painful as their lives may be, they still can choose to heal their heart, mind, soul and have a joyful, purposeful and peaceful life. The bereaved can be encouraged to do the following:

- ***Healing the Mind*** comes when the bereaved are willing to accept their new identity and purpose. Ask them how death has changed their self-perception and what do they want to do with the rest of their life. Encourage them to think positively.
- ***Healing the Heart*** happens when the bereaved are willing to reinvest their emotional energy into new tasks, relationships, hobbies, and other things. Ask the bereaved to list some things that they can do to make themselves feel happy.
- ***Healing the Soul*** occurs when the bereaved develop a new meaning in life. The Pastor, Chaplain or Deacon can help them develop a vision for themselves which *may* mean discussing a change in career, long range planning, new housing, dating again, moving, Last Will and Testament, developing their spiritual life, learning to appreciate life more, spending more time with family and friends, and getting in touch with their passion. [38]

LOGOTHERAPY

Many seniors are struggling with life's meaning and purpose. At one point in their lives, they were married, raising children, going to work and doing many fulfilling activities. However, their life has dramatically changed. Some may feel lonely because their spouse has died, and the children are grown and left home. Some feel bored because they are retired and have nothing of value to do. The aging process, and physical illness has restricted their mobility so they unable to do what they used to do. Unfortunately, some of our aging adults live bored, empty lives and are not experiencing the "golden years". They need a new purpose and vision in life.

Logo therapy or reflective conversation can help them to rediscover a new meaning in life and age gracefully. Logo therapy was developed by the renowned neurologist and psychiatrist Viktor Frankl who was a survivor of a Nazi concentration camp. He discovered that people can overcome pain, suffering and death when they have a reason to live. Frankl believed that striving to find meaning in life is the primary, powerful motivating and driving force in humans. In Frankl's' *Will to Meaning* he shares these basic tenets:

- Life has meaning even in painful, difficult circumstances
- Our primary purpose for living is our will to find meaning in life
- We have freedom to find meaning in what we do and what we experience or at least in the stand we take when faced with a situation of unchangeable suffering. [39]

Seniors need to understand they still have the freedom to choose how they will respond to life's hardships and develop a new purpose in life. They may have lost their health, loved ones, mobility, career, family life however, they never lose what Frankl calls the "Final Freedom" which is the freedom to choose how to respond to life's circumstances.

Logo therapy is an excellent spiritual intervention or tool to assist seniors in developing a new purpose and a positive perspective. Asking the right questions can unlock the doors of spiritual insight and understanding. It can raise the conscious level of seniors and make them learn more about themselves and God. They will discover what is important to them and what they still can do to have a meaningful life. They can rediscover their latent gifts, talents and skills and enjoy their life.

Logo therapy or reflective conversation can open the mind to a positive perspective, sensitize the heart to its hidden passions, and inspire the soul with new meaning and purpose.

Logo therapy can give the elderly a whole new perspective and enable them to cope with their losses. They can choose to see their pain and suffering as an opportunity for spiritual growth. Instead of wallowing in despair, they can choose to have hope. Instead of complaining to God for what they do not have, they can praise God for what they do have.

Seniors can be taught to have a positive attitude and be grateful in all circumstances. New insights, pearls of wisdom and development of character can come from reflecting on painful experiences. Logo therapy assist seniors in finding the redemptive purpose to their afflictions and adversities. [40]

The Spiritual Care Provider, Pastor, Deacon, Chaplain, Physicians, lay person, Social Worker and caregivers can ask reflective questions to help aging adults to develop a new purpose in their life. They can assist them in creating goals and a vision which recognizes their gifts and current abilities. Also, the spiritual care provider can remind seniors of their inner strength and wisdom to make decisions for themselves. The following reflective questions can be asked:

- What can you do to make life meaningful?
- What can you still do to enjoy your life?
- What kind of attitude do you need to cope with your situation?
- What messages do you want to give your loved ones?
- What is your legacy?
- What is it you can do to cope with your loss?
- How can sickness and suffering strengthen or develop your character?
- What wisdom have you learned from your painful past experiences?
- How can a positive attitude help you?

There is a story of a sixty-five-year old terminally ill man in his home. He discovered he was going to die and was extremely depressed.

He was so full of despair that he shunned all visitors, stayed locked up in his bedroom, and kept all lights off and blinds closed. His room seemed like a dungeon. There was an atmosphere of hopelessness in the room. His family insisted that I, his pastor, visit him. I visited him, and he barely said anything. We sat in silence for a long time.

He broke the silence and said with anger, "It's not fair. It's not fair. I am a Christian. I pray and what good is it? Why am I dying? Why am I suffering? Why is this happening to me?"

I shared with him that I did not have any good answers to his questions. However, I did make this statement: "None of us know how long we will live. Any of us could die at any time. So, the question is not when are you going to die? The question is what will you do in the meantime? We cannot add more days to our lives, but we can add more life to our days. What are you going to do?"

We began to reflect on the things he could still do. When I returned to see him, a major transformation had taken place. The lights were not only on in his room, but they were on his life. He was hopeful and joyful and had a new meaning in his life. The dreary, dark room had been transformed into a sanctuary of praise and hope. He had gospel music playing on the radio. The blinds were open. He had a bible on his bed, and he was singing to the glory of God.

I asked him, "What happened?" He said he was reflecting on his life and what he could still do. He exclaimed, "I don't know when I am going to die, but I know that I can still praise and thank God for the life I still have, and I can still teach my children and grandchildren how to live and how to die." Because of our reflective conversation, this grandfather found a reason to live. [41]

CHAPTER 4

Spiritual Care Support Group for Aging Adults

"And it is still true, no matter how old you are, when you go out into the world it is best to hold hands and stick together." – Robert Fulghum, author

A Spiritual Care Support Group consists of all seniors and it provides them the opportunity to express their thoughts, feelings, beliefs, opinions, and spiritual concerns in a non-judgmental, non-religious, non-threatening, nurturing, empowering, and enlightening environment. Spiritual Care Support is *not* religious care or worship, even though the group may address religious issues. However, the purpose of the Spiritual Care Support Group is to address the spiritual needs of aging adults, enhance their spirituality and encourage their spiritual practices.

The Pastor, Chaplain, Deacon, lay person, Recreational Therapist, or Social Worker will ensure that the environment is conducive to spiritual discussions by suggesting the following ground rules.

- Every person is entitled to their own views and beliefs and has the right to express or not express them
- Every person must not judge or criticize another person's views or beliefs

- Spiritual Care Group should not be used to proselytize anyone's religion or philosophy.
- No one should monopolize the discussion. Everyone is encouraged to share
- Everyone is responsible to discover the spiritual meaning for themselves
- Persons who share confidential information will be encouraged to meet privately with the Chaplain, Pastor or Social Worker *after* the group meeting
- Every person is encouraged to speak positively and encourage one another.

I have led Spiritual Care Support Groups at PACE of Southeast Michigan and these groups have increased their spiritual wellness. Also, Friendship Baptist Church, Ms. Maxine McBride, Mrs. Catherine Clark and I developed a Senior Support Group that meets once a month. The Senior Support Group provides spiritual messages, health information, a nurturing fellowship and socio-cultural outings. It is a wonderful group where religious seniors age gracefully. I highly recommend that every Pastor or Deacon develop a Senior Support Group.

SPIRITUAL CARE SUPPORT GROUP SURVEY

The Spiritual Care Provider, Pastor, Deacon, Chaplain, lay person, or Social Worker may want to do a survey and discover what the senior's religious or spiritual interest. It is especially important that a Nursing home and assisted living facility be given a *Spiritual Care Support Group Survey* to determine the spiritual needs or interest of the elderly. Special attention needs to be given to elderly persons who may have difficulty writing or comprehending the survey. Once it is filled out, the facilitator will be able to prepare him or herself on issues that the aging adults want to discuss. The following *Spiritual Care Support Group Survey* can be implemented.

SPIRITUAL CARE SUPPORT GROUP SURVEY

1. ***What spiritual virtues or religious practices do you want to discuss? (Circle all that apply)***
   Faith Hope Love Peace Forgiveness Joy God Sanctification Praise Mindfulness Spirituality Meditation Prayer Worship Service Holidays Other

2. ***What religion would you like to discuss or know more about?***
   Christianity Judaism Buddhism Islam Jehovah Witness Catholicism New Age Spirituality Pentecostalism Baptist Methodist Lutheranism Episcopal Bible Koran Agnosticism Humanism Other

3. ***What spiritual needs do you want to discuss?***
   Grief and loss Death and Dying Painful Past Failure Finances Faith Overcoming Adversity Spiritual Growth Forgiveness Sin Guilt Anger Sadness Loneliness Hopelessness Faults Finite Family
   Doubt Worry Fear Relationships Addictions Sexuality Goals Lack of spirituality Procrastination End of life issues Family Feelings
   Past transgressions Meaning and purpose Other _____

4. ***What are some other topics or issues that you would like to discuss?***

The *Spiritual Care Survey* is very instrumental in letting one know the religious and spiritual concerns of the elderly. The Chaplain, Pastor, Recreational Therapist, or Social Worker can develop Spiritual Wellness topics. Moreover, they can facilitate discussions on contemporary issues, media, politics, poetry, grief issues, life review, spiritual coping skills, religion, philosophy, sacred writings, books, famous quotes, various beliefs, music, feelings, faults, focuses, finances, family, and the finite. Hopefully, each topic will provoke a vibrant conversation in which they can share their thoughts and feelings and understand its spiritual implications.

SPIRITUAL WELLNESS TOPICS

The following Spiritual Wellness Topics were derived from the elderly participants of the PACE program of South East Michigan which serves over seven hundred elderly participants. Each of these Spiritual Wellness topics begins with an opening statement, followed by discussion questions and an ending statement. The emphasis should always be getting people to share their thoughts and feelings. As the Spiritual Care Coordinator for the PACE program, I facilitated lively discussions with forty to sixty elderly participants on the following topics:

1. FORGIVENESS
2. LOVE
3. HOPE
4. PEACE
5. JOY
6. HEALING YOUR GRIEVING
7. DR MARTIN LUTHER KING
8. WHO IS GOD TO YOU?
9. DO NOT GO GENTLE INTO THAT GOOD NIGHT
10. STROLL DOWN MEMORY LANE
11. CARPE DIEM
12. THANKSGIVING
13. NEVER TOO OLD
14. AGING GRACEFULLY
15. STILL I RISE

SPIRITUAL WELLNESS TOPIC: *FORGIVENESS*

OPENING STATEMENT:

Many wise men have written about forgiveness. Mahatma Ghandi wrote, "The weak can never forgive. Forgiveness is the attribute of the strong." Jesus Christ warned us, "For if ye forgive men their trespasses, your Heavenly Father will also forgive you." (Matthew 6:14 - KJV)

These are powerful words of wisdom. Unfortunately, for many people it's hard to forgive. Forgiveness is not easy, especially when you have been hurt by a family member or close friend. Consequently, we hold onto a lot of anger, bitterness, vindictiveness and even hatred.

DISCUSSION QUESTIONS:

Why is it so hard to forgive?
Why is unforgiveness bad for us?
How do you think unforgiveness affect us physically?
How do you think unforgiveness affects us emotionally?
How do you think unforgiveness affects us spiritually?
What do you think the benefits are in forgiving someone?

CLOSING STATEMENT:

Bernard Meltzer is right, "When you forgive, you in no way change the past- but you sure do change the future." You can change your future by forgiving everyone of everything they say and did to you. You can let go of all the anger, bitterness and vengefulness of the past and experience inner peace and love. You can experience peace of mind if you forgive others.

SPIRITUAL WELLNESS TOPIC:
LOVE

OPENING STATEMENT:

It has been said that the greatest commandment is "Thou shalt love the Lord thy God with all thy heart, and with all thy soul, and with all thy mind." (Matthew 22:37- KJV) There is nothing more powerful than love. Love can transform a foe into a friend and inspire peace and justice in the world. Love can heal a broken heart, cleanse a sinful soul and give peace of mind that surpasses all understanding. Love puts a smile on our face, pep in our step and thanksgiving on our lips. Thomas Merton once wrote, "Love seeks one thing only: the good of the one loved. It leaves all the other secondary effects to take care of themselves. Love, therefore is its own reward."

DISCUSSION QUESTIONS:

Why is it so important to love people?
Why is it important to love God?
Why is it important to love yourself?
What are somethings you could to love yourself?
What are somethings you could do to love God?
What are somethings you could to love others?

CLOSING STATEMENT:

George Sand is right, "There is only one happiness in life, to love and be loved." If you really want to be happy, if you want peace of mind, serve and help others. Being caring and giving is the path to prosperity, peace and joy. Love yourself, respect yourself and you'll be able to love and respect others.

SPIRITUAL WELLNESS TOPIC:
HOPE

OPENING STATEMENT:

Bishop Desmond Tutu once said, "Hope is being able to see that there is light despite all of the darkness." When a person loses hope they find it difficult to see goodness in themselves, in people and in the future. They tend to focus on the negative instead of the positive. One of the ways we keep a sense of hope is by looking past the darkness of despair to see the light.

DISCUSSION QUESTIONS:

Where do you see the goodness of God?
What gives you hope and why?
Where do you see the "light" or hope in your life?
How does God give you hope?
Describe the difference between a person who has hope and a person who has despair?
What kind of a person are you? Are you a person of hope or despair and why?

CLOSING STATEMENT

A person of hope is someone who chooses to have a positive attitude rather than a negative one. It is someone who sees the light instead of the darkness. They believe that all things are possible with God. They never give up, never throw in the towel. They keep on fighting, believing, serving, loving, praying and doing good.

SPIRITUAL WELLNESS TOPIC:
PEACE

OPENING STATEMENT:

Henry David Thoreau said, "The masses of men live lives of quiet desperation." Many people desperately seek peace of mind. Some people are worried and preoccupied with paying bills and making the ends meet. Others lack peace of mind because of their fears. They are afraid of being a victim of a crime, contracting a terminal illness or being in a tragic accident. Those persons who are grieving the death of a loved one or a broken relationship are robbed of peace. Their tears blind them of life's joys. People who are ill or physically challenged may lack peace. All the medication and physicians in the world has not given them enough comfort. Some people are always trying to control others and they lack peace. Others, thinking negatively has stripped them of serenity. There are many things that rob us of peace of mind.

DISCUSSION QUESTIONS:

What or who disturbs your peace?
What do you do or say that takes away your peace?
What could you do to have peace of mind?

CLOSING STATEMENT:

One of the ways to obtain peace of mind is by talking, thinking and praying to God. The Bible states, "Thou wilt keep him in perfect peace whose mind is stayed on thee." (Isaiah 26:3-KJV) The most therapeutic thing we could do is pray. When we pray to God, we can share all our fears, frustrations, worries, sadness and doubts and He gives us peace of mind that surpasses all understanding.

SPIRITUAL WELLNESS TOPIC:
JOY

OPENING STATEMENT:

Abraham Lincoln said, "People are as happy as they want to be." In other words, happiness is a choice, it is a positive attitude. Happiness is a positive perspective, emphasizing good instead of evil; hope instead of despair. It is up to you to decide if you want to experience happiness. No one or nothing can upset you unless you allow them to. You must make a conscious decision to be happy.

DISCUSSION QUESTIONS:

What can you do to make yourself happy?
How does positive thinking make you happy?
What are you looking forward to doing?
What makes you smile?

CLOSING STATEMENT:

We need to be happy for this moment. This moment is your life. This is the only day that we have. We cannot afford to take life for granted. Happiness is not something that we delay for the future. It is something that we enjoy in the present. Happiness lies in our ability to find something to be grateful for and extract the positive from the negative.

SPIRITUAL WELLNESS TOPIC: *HEALING YOUR GRIEVING*

OPENING STATEMENT:

Grief is a natural, physical, emotional and spiritual personal experience to death and loss. Grief can express itself in profound sadness, shock, confusion, anger, despair, guilt, disorientation, helplessness, loneliness, emptiness and bewilderment. We all grieve and we all grieve in our own way.

DISCUSSION QUESTIONS:

Who are you in grief about? When did they die and how do you feel?
What do you miss most about your loved one?
What do you do to cope with your grief?

CLOSING STATEMENT:

The Bible states, "Blessed are they that mourn for they shall be comforted." (Matthew 5:4-NRSV) One of the major ways in which we are healed is by embracing and expressing our grief. The more we shed our tears the more we are healed. Scientist have discovered that 40% of our emotional pain is relieved when we cry, therefore, if we want to be healed of our grief shed some tears. Give yourself time to grieve. Share your grief with a Chaplain, Social Worker, Pastor, family member, close friend or journal your thoughts and feelings. The more you grieve, the more you will heal.

SPIRITUAL WELLNESS TOPIC:
DR. MARTIN LUTHER KING, JR.

OPENING STATEMENT:

America has a national holiday for a great African American, preacher, civil rights leader, non-violent warrior, Noble Peace prize winner Dr. Martin Luther King Jr. Dr. King and a multitude of clergy, civil rights workers, freedom fighters, humanitarians and people of good will marched, protested, engaged in civil disobedience, and boycotts to end racial segregation and pass civil rights legislation. Dr. King was unjustly arrested 22 times, harassed by the FBI, vilified by White clergy, ostracized by Black Militants, alienated by conservative Black clergy, endure death threats, his house was fire bombed, he was stabbed at a Book signing, and assassinated at Hotel. Despite of the persecution, pain and suffering, Dr. King continued to pursue his Dream, taking some of the hypocrisy out of American democracy.

DISCUSSION QUESTIONS:

What are your memories of Dr. King?
What was it like to live during the civil rights movement?
What do you appreciate about Dr. King?
What is the best way to remember Dr. King's birthday?

CLOSING STATEMENT

We should thank and praise God for Dr. Martin Luther King. If it were not for the sacrifices of Dr. King, we would not experience many civil and human rights that we tend to take for granted. We would still be sitting in the back of the bus, denied the right to vote, be insulted by Jim Crow signs, denied employment and educational opportunities. If it were not for Dr. King there would not be an Oprah Winfrey, Beyoncé, Kevin Hart or President Barak Obama. We should take time to reflect on the life and legacy of Dr. King.

SPIRITUAL WELLNESS TOPIC: *WHO IS GOD TO YOU?*

OPENING STATEMENT:

Who is God to you? God is called a lot of names. The Muslims refer to God as Allah. The Quakers call him The Light. The Jewish people refer to God as Yahweh translated as Jehovah. The seven names of God in the Old Testament are *Jehovah Jireh*-The Lord will provide, *Jehovah Rapha* – The Lord that healeth, Jehovah Nissi-The Lord is our Banner and *Jehovah Roha*- the Lord my Shepard and *Jehovah Shalom* – the Lord is my Peace. These names were ascribed to God based on what God has done for the people. What do you call God and what has God done for you? Everyone has the right to their beliefs.

DISCUSSION QUESTIONS:

What do you call God and why?
Who is God to you?
What has God done for you?

CLOSING STATEMENT:

Your faith and belief in God is important. It determines your spiritual, emotional and physical wellbeing. One of the more popular titles about God is found in the 23rd Psalm. "The Lord is my Shepard I shall not want." (Psalm 23:1-KJV) For David, God was a Shepard who fulfilled his emotional, spiritual and physical needs. If you have a personal relationship with God, you will be content and satisfied with your life. You will not need anything and anybody. God will heal your broken heart, ease your troubled mind and fulfill your empty soul.

SPIRITUAL WELLNESS TOPIC: *DO NOT GO GENTLE INTO THAT GOOD NIGHT*

OPENING STATEMENT:

A Welsh poet named Dylan Thomas wrote these immortal words for his dying father, *"Do not go gentle into that good night..."* To rage against the dying light is to struggle and strive against the dying process. It means to live your life to the fullest and not let the threat of death discourage you. We must have the faith to face our fears and do as much as we can.

DISCUSSION QUESTIONS:

How do you feel about dying?
What kind of attitude do you want to have as you confront death?
What do you think happens when you die?
Have you made your peace with your God?
What "unfinished business" do you have?
Have you prepared your Last Will and Testament?
If the doctor said, "You have 6 months to live", what would you do?

CLOSING STATEMENT:

We are not guaranteed to live the next 6 months, 6 weeks, or 6 days. We are not promised to live next week or even tomorrow. Therefore, we must live each day as if it is our last. Celebrate every moment, be thankful for life's little blessings, worship God, express your love, and pursue your dreams. You possess an unconquerable spirit that defies pain, sickness, suffering and death. Do not go gentle into that good night, Rage, rage against the dying light.

SPIRITUAL WELLNESS TOPIC: *STROLL DOWN MEMORY LANE*

OPENING STATEMENT:

The poet Loretta Hitch wrote a poem called, *"Stroll Down Memory."* Every now and then we need to stroll down memory lane. Our memories are precious because they represent our collective history, our identity, and the accumulation of our experiences. Memories are anchored in personal, cultural and social experiences. Moreover, they throw new light on our past, remind us of the presence of God and foster a sense of gratitude. Taking a stroll down memory lane counteracts loneliness, boredom and anxiety- making life seem more meaningful and death less frightening.

DISCUSSION QUESTIONS:

What is your favorite memory, that puts a smile on your face?
What is your greatest memory as a child, teenager or youth?
What was your mother or father like?
What was your favorite TV show, or Movie? (*Lucy, Andy Griffith, Gone with the Wind, Wizard of Oz, Ed Sullivan Show, Imitation of Life, 10 Commandments*)
What was your favorite soloist or Band? (*Temptations, Stevie Wonder, Cab Calloway, B.B. King, Johnnie Cash, Beatles, Elvis Pressley*)

CLOSING STATEMENT:

We need to take a stroll down memory lane and enjoy ourselves. It is good to look at old pictures and reminisce. It will bring a smile on your face and peace in your soul. Why don't you take a stroll down memory lane?

SPIRITUAL WELLNESS TOPIC:
CARPE DIEM

OPENING STATEMENT:

The Roman poet Horace used the Latin expression *Carpe Diem*. It literally means "Pluck the day" and it is usually translated "Seize the day". In other words, we must make the most of our present time. We must seize the pleasures of the moment without concern for the future. We cannot waste time or take life for granted. We must live as if we were to die tomorrow. Do not wait for something to happen, make it happen. Do not wait for extraordinary opportunities, seize common occasions and make them special.

DISCUSSION QUESTIONS:

Is there something that you need to do today?
What could you do *today* to change your life?
What else could you *today* to enjoy your life?
What dream do you need to pursue?
Who do you need to give more love to?
What could you do *today* to experience peace of mind?

CLOSING STATEMENT:

Buddha once said, "The trouble is you think you have time." We cannot afford to waste time. Tomorrow is not promised to any of us. We could die on any given day; therefore, we must seize the day. Mark Twain tells us, "Life is short. Break the rules, forgive quickly. Kiss slowly. Love truly. Laugh uncontrollably and never regret anything that makes you smile." Seize the day!!

SPIRITUAL WELLNESS TOPIC: *THANKSGIVING*

OPENING STATEMENT:

Thanksgiving Day is a national holiday commemorated on the fourth Thursday of November. This is the time when families come together, express their gratitude and enjoy a delicious feast. It is a wonderful holiday. A time of love, laughter, food, football, family and fun. It is a time to reflect and give thanks on all of life's' blessings.

DISCUSSION QUESTIONS:

What are you thankful for?
How has God blessed you?
What are you thankful for about your family?
What are you thankful for about your job or retirement?
What do you thank and praise God for?

CLOSING STATEMENT:

The Bible commands, "Forget not His benefits." (Psalm 103:2-KJV) We should never forget what God has done for us. It was God who fed, clothed, healed, protected and provided for us. We should thank God, every morning and say, "This is the day that the Lord has made let us rejoice and be glad in it." We should express our appreciation to each other. Let us not wait until Thanksgiving or the Holidays before we tell people we love them. Give people their roses now while they can smell them.

SPIRITUAL WELLNESS TOPIC: *NEVER TOO OLD*

OPENING STATEMENT

Les Brown the motivator once wrote, "You are never too old to set another goal or to dream a new dream." As long as you are alive, blood courses through your veins, and your name is not in the obituary column, you have something to do. It does not matter how old you are, there is still a lot you can accomplish. Your body may be weak, your vision blurred, and gait slow, you still can achieve remarkable things. You are never too old to achieve a goal, move a mountain, and fulfill a dream. Many aging adults were able to do the impossible. The octogenarian Abraham and Sarah had enough faith to produce their first child Isaac. Moses was in his 80s' when he liberated his people from Egyptian bondage and Joshua led the Jewish people into the Promise land when he was in his 70s'. Colonial Sanders was in his 88 when he made "finger licking good chicken". Ed Krock created the Big Mack when he was in his 70s. An 80-year-old Harriett Tubman out dodged, out strategize, and outran the Klu, Klux Klan and freed over 300 slaves via the Underground railroad. You are never too old because with God *all* things are possible!

DISCUSSION QUESTIONS:

What is your vision for the future?
What is it that you can still do?
What goal(s) do you want to accomplish?

CLOSING STATEMENT:

You are never too old to live out your dreams. Your faith in God and in yourself will compensate for your physical weakness. The body gets weak, but the soul is strong enough to do the will of God. There is still a lot of good work you can do. You may be retired from the workforce but not from service to God and humanity. You can still offer prayer, words of wisdom, mentoring, service and leadership.

SPIRITUAL WELLNESS TOPIC: *AGING GRACEFULLY*

OPENING STATEMENT:

The immortal movie actress Bette Davis once said, "Old age is not for sissies." Her humorous point was there are a lot of physical, emotional, psychological, spiritual and financial challenges in the aging process. As we grow older the body naturally deteriorates and we are susceptible to all kinds of illness, weaknesses and diseases. Moreover, the deaths of family and friends presents an emotional and psychological challenge. Also, being retired, feeling bored with limited resources can be a spiritual and financial struggle.

DISCUSSION QUESTIONS:

What are your challenges?
What can a person do to cope with their challenges?
What do you think it means to age gracefully?

CLOSING STATEMENT:

Despite all the losses that we experience in life there are some things that we never lose. We never lose our ability to respond to our circumstances. We have the freedom to choose our attitude, perspective and beliefs. We can choose to age gracefully if we choose to have faith, hope and love. *Faith* in yourself is what you need to handle the daily struggles. *Hope* in God is needed to believe in the future. Never stop hoping and believing that things will get better. Finally, *love* God and yourself and others makes life meaningful. Worship God, love your neighbor and most importantly love yourself. If you have faith, hope and love you will age gracefully.

SPIRITUAL WELLNESS TOPIC:
STILL I RISE

OPENING STATEMENT:

The renowned poet Laurette Maya Angelou penned a powerful, inspirational poem entitled, *"Still I Rise."*

DISCUSSION QUESTIONS:

- What does it mean to rise spiritually?
- What does it mean to rise emotionally?
- How does a positive, hopeful attitude help you to rise above adversity?
- What could you do to improve your life?

CLOSING STATEMENT:

Still I rise, should be the motto on everyone's lips. Despite life's trials and tribulations – *Still I rise*. There is absolutely nothing in this world that can keep you down or destroy you. You have an indomitable, indestructible soul that cannot be broken or defeated by the adversities and afflictions of life. God will resurrect your soul every time someone or something attempts to suppress it. Every time life knocks you down, your soul shall rise again so that you may say, *"Still I Rise."*

CHAPTER 5

Spiritual Values for Aging Adults

"Virtue is more to a man than either water or fire. I have seen men die from treading on water and fire, but I have never seen a man die from treading the course of virtue." – Confucius

"He who sows virtue reaps glory." – Leonardo Da Vinci

Aging gracefully is the transformation and beautification of the soul through the acceptance and application of spiritual values. There are six spiritual values that aging adults need to age gracefully, and they are peace, faith, hope, love, joy and grace. To practice these spiritual virtues fosters healing for the soul, strength to the spirit and peace of mind. Aging gracefully depends upon the senior's ability to use these values as a way of life.

"Aging is a self-fulfilling prophecy," says Walter Bortz, MD, Stanford University School of Medicine professor and author of *Living Longer for Dummies and Dare to be 100*. According to Bortz, the most crucial factor in aging gracefully is cultivating a positive outlook. Research shows that your attitude, resiliency and the way you cope with stress may be predictors of healthy aging than physical disease or disability.

"It's not how old you are, it's how you are old."- Jules Renard

Aging adults who desire to age gracefully can adopt a positive perspective and attitude based on peace, faith, hope, love, joy and grace. These spiritual values are universal and can be practiced by everyone regardless of race, class, sexual orientation, educational background and religion.

Aging gracefully is the transformation and beautification of the soul through the acceptance and application of spiritual values.

PEACE

Aging gracefully requires seniors to develop a sense of peace. The Greek word for peace is *kirene* which means contentment, wholeness and satisfaction. The Hebrew translation for peace is *Shalom* which is peace amid pain, suffering and evil. God gives us peace that surpasses all understanding. No one or nothing can disrupt your peace of mind unless you allow it.

Many aging adults desire peace. They are at a point in their lives when they want peace and quiet in their home. They eschew the changes, chaos and confusion of their youth. The want peace of mind to cope with the changes of their golden years.

Peace comes with accepting the unacceptable and tolerating the intolerable. Seniors must cease from trying to control people and situations and trust God. *They must learn to let go and let God.* Isaiah the prophet reminds us, "Thou wilt give Him perfect peace whose mind is stayed on thee." (Isaiah 26:3-KJV) Focus more on God than yourself or problems and discover His peace. Pray and tell all your fears, frustrations, anxieties, troubles and sorrows to God and experience inner tranquility. Peace comes when we commune with the God of peace. When we pray and accept our new reality with its limitations and losses, we will experience an inner tranquility which will enable us to age gracefully. To foster a sense of peace, do the following:

- Pray for peace. Share all your feelings and thoughts to God
- Cease from trying to control people or situations. Accept the unacceptable

- Focus on positive thoughts and not negative thoughts

FAITH

Faith in God and in oneself is required to age gracefully. The Greek word for faith is *pistos* which means ultimate trust. We must place our faith, and complete trust and dependence on God. The Bible states, "the just shall live by faith." (Hab. 2:4-KJV) Faith is not a doctrine or belief, it is a way of life. It is the belief that God is working through you and with you. The elderly need to cultivate this kind of faith to get through arduous physical therapy sessions, cope with illness, overcome adversities, live a productive life and age gracefully. To strengthen your faith, do the following:

- Read positive thoughts and sacred texts
- Speak encouraging words to yourself
- Believe in yourself
- Believe in God

HOPE

Hope in God and in the future, is essential to aging gracefully. Hope is what gives life meaning and purpose. It inspires you to pursue your dreams. C.S. Lewis is right, "You are never too old to set another goal or to dream a new dream." Seniors who have a vision for themselves, feel good about themselves and their future. Even if their dreams are deferred, they believe that "all things work together for good to those who love God and called according to His purpose." (Romans 8:28-KJV) Seniors with hope believe that things will work out in their favor. They let their "hopes, not their hurts, shape their future", states Robert Schuller. To develop a sense of hope, do the following:

- Write a vision for yourself and pursue it
- Create a to do list
- Develop a new meaning or purpose in life
- Create a Goal and work to achieve it
- Ask yourself, "What do I want to accomplish in life?"

LOVE

Loving God, your neighbor and yourself is a necessary requirement to aging gracefully. The Greek word for Love is *Agape* which is the love of God working in the human heart. The elderly must learn to give love and receive love. Moreover, they must learn to love themselves. Jenn Proske wrote, "Love yourself. It is important to stay positive because beauty comes from the inside out." When we learn to love and respect ourselves we age gracefully. To cultivate the virtue of love, do the following:

- Speak positively to yourself and never put yourself down
- Look into the mirror and tell yourself. "I love you."
- Worship, praise and express your love to God
- Do what makes you feel good
- Avoid or ignore people who are negative and bring your spirit down
- Forgive yourself of your sins and shortcomings
- Respect and appreciate your strengths and weaknesses and be yourself
- Do not participate in anything that goes against your moral conscience
- Express your love to family and friends
- Be willing to serve and help others, especially those in need
- Share your gift, talents, experiences with others and do not seek compensation

JOY

Experiencing joy and laughter is essential to aging gracefully. "The joy we feel has little to do with the circumstances of our lives and everything to do with the focus of our lives", states Russel M. Nelson. Seniors who focus their joy on God, and positive things in life will experience joy. They understand that is in the giving that they receive and "the joy of the Lord is their strength." (Nehemiah 8:10-KJV) Joy is a positive attitude that grins in the face of defeat and defies the odds. It is an unconquerable spirit that always finds something positive in a negative situation. Seniors who choose joy over sorrow and laughter over lamentation will age gracefully. The following tips will foster your sense of joy:

- Reflect over your life and praise God for healing, saving, protecting, delivering and blessing you
- Keep a positive attitude
- Count your blessings
- Choose to be joyful, have fun
- Find something to laugh about
- Make others laugh, it is medicine for the soul
- Do what makes you smile or gives you peace

GRACE

Grace is desperately needed to age gracefully. Grace is Gods' unmerited favor. It cannot be earned, achieved or worked for. Grace is something that is given free from God. Grace compensates for our transgressions, weaknesses, faults and failures. Grace helps us to accept our imperfections and the imperfections of others. We can agree with the wise words of Rick Warren, "What gives me the most hope every day is God's grace; knowing that his grace is going to give me the strength for whatever I face, knowing that nothing is a surprise to God." Gods' grave is mercy, love, longsuffering, tolerance and patience.

Seniors need Gods' grace to cope with life's sudden changes and challenges. Life is so unpredictable, and we are all very vulnerable. It takes God's grace to cope with the death of loved ones, illness, change, loss and the aging process. We must learn Reinhold Niebuhr's prayer, *"God grant me the serenity to accept the things I cannot change the courage to change the things I can, and the wisdom to know the difference."* When we accept Gods' grace and mercy will inevitably age gracefully. The following suggestions will assist you with Gods' grace.

- Accept the fact that no one is perfect, including yourself
- Forgive people and don't hold onto grudges
- Understand that God loves you and accepts you with your flaws
- Accept the fact that you must be willing to change and be flexible

Seniors do not have to go gentle into that good night. We do not have to surrender to the inevitability of illness and death. We can choose to have an unconquerable and unbreakable spirit. Believing and practicing peace, faith, hope, love, joy and grace will empower us to fight against the dying light.

The writer has used these Spiritual Virtues for religious seniors and spiritual seniors with remarkable success. In my twenty-three years as a Pastor of Friendship Baptist Church, sixteen years as a Hospice Chaplain for Henry Ford, and being the Spiritual Care Coordinator for over 650 elderly participants of the PACE of Southeast Michigan, I have discovered that elderly persons who practiced these Spiritual Values age gracefully.

CHAPTER 6

Spiritual Self-Care for Caregivers and Healthcare Providers

"Self-care is so important. When you take time to replenish your spirit, it allows you to serve others from the overflow. You cannot serve from an empty vessel." – Eleanor Brown

Caring for aging adults can be emotionally draining, psychologically destabilizing and spiritually depleting. Physicians, Caregivers, Health aides, Clergy, Social Workers, Nurses, Recreational therapist, Geriatric workers, and Nursing home workers can all suffer from burn out. Burnout is what happens when we ignore the spiritual needs of the soul. We can be so preoccupied with caring for others that we neglect to care for ourselves. It does not matter how young, healthy or holy we are, we all can suffer from burnout. This is especially true, for caregivers who live with elderly family members suffering from dementia, Alzheimer's and or a terminal illness.

CAUSES OF BURN OUT/ SELF-CARE TIPS

Burn out is a physical, mental and emotional exhaustion. It can lead to dulled emotions and detachment. It deteriorates our feelings and undermines motivation, leaving a sense of hopelessness. Kristina Ericksen a Content Marketing Specialist at the College of Education for Rasmussen College shares several factors that lead to burn out. [42]

1. **Putting others first**

When we put the needs of others before our own we will burn ourselves out. It is hard to say no to people we love or care about. We may even feel guilty when we take care of ourselves, however, it is unhealthy to love others and not yourself.

2. **Long Shifts**

Health care professionals who work long shifts and can suffer from severe fatigue. Also, caregivers who live with their elderly loved ones do not get a day off. They are there all the time caring for their every need. It is natural for them to feel exhausted and overwhelmed.

3. **Busy high-stress environments**

Health care professionals have a lot on their plates. The high demands for documentation, short staffing problems, and extensive work load leads to burn out. A stressful home can burn out caregivers who must juggle many responsibilities. Some work a fulltime job, raise children, pay the bills, cook meals, clean the house, be a supportive spouse and care for their elderly parent. At the end of the day they are drained.

4. **Dealing with Sickness and Death**

Being constantly exposed to illness and loss can take its toll on our emotional wellbeing. Emotional baggage and grief can creep into our soul and depress us.

Are you burned out? Are you under a lot of stress? Are you

emotionally and physically drained? Is it getting harder and harder to function because you are so tired? Did you ever get so overwhelmed and frustrated that you lashed out in anger? Is it hard for you to watch your loved one slowly deteriorate? Do feel sad because of the senseless pain and suffering?

"My caregiver mantra is to remember 'The only control you have is over the changes you choose to make." – Nancy L. Kriseman

Do you feel as if you are taking care of everyone else but yourself? Are you physically exhausted and unable to meet the constant demands of your loved one? If you are feeling burned out, take heed to the following self-care tips:

CAREGIVING COPING SKILLS

1. **Set boundaries**

You must learn how to say no to safeguard your wellbeing. Set boundaries on your commitments both in and out of the workplace to avoid overextending yourself.

2. **Process your emotions**

Find a good listener who you can leave your emotional baggage at work instead of bringing it at home at the end of the day. Or speak to a friend therapist, counselor or clergy person.

3. **Put yourself first**

Devote a certain amount of time every day to focus on yourself. Prioritize your mental health and schedule intentional time to relax and unwind. Do something just for the sake of enjoyment.

4. **Manage your stress**

Addressing your stress instead of ignoring it can help combat burn out. Be deliberate in your actions whether that's through exercise, health eating or meditation. Control your outlook through positive, intentional thoughts.

5. **Find solace in creativity**

Pick up an old hobby or try to do something new. Be it painting, writing or trying out a new recipe, keeping your hands busy can help you reflect and sort out your emotions. [43]

SPIRITUAL SELF-CARE COPING SKILLS

Spiritual Self-Care Coping Skills can assist you with the emotional, psychological and spiritual symptoms of burn out. These Spiritual Coping Skills will bring healing and restoration to your heart, mind and soul.

"One goal of the mindful caregiver is to find ways to not feel 'dis-eased' in the caregiving process." – Nancy L. Kriseman

Spiritual Coping Skills can guard your soul from being dis-eased and burned out. I would strongly suggest you use the following Spiritual Coping Skills: prayer, praise, positive thinking, purposefulness, and pampering yourself.

PRAYER

Prayer is a dialogue between a person of faith and their God. It is sharing your thoughts, and feelings to a compassionate God who hears and answers prayer. Prayer is therapeutic, in that the more a person expresses their anger, fear, frustration, doubt, despair, sadness, hopelessness and emptiness, the more they'll experience divine healing. Prayer gives us the spiritual strength in times of weakness. Soren

Kierkegaard is right, "Prayer does not change God, but it changes him who prays." Talk to God and God will heal and strengthen you.

PRAISE

Praising God or expressing our gratitude is essential to our spiritual wellbeing. Thanking God for all of life's blessings eradicates the bitterness and resentment in our soul. The more we count our blessings, the better we feel about our life. Praise gives glory to God and opens us up to a deeper union with Him. It turns our attention off our problems and on the goodness of God. Praise God when you minister to an aging adult. Thank Him for the privilege of service and all the things He has done for you. Praise God for all the things He has done through you.

POSITIVE THINKING

Positive thinking is a mental attitude manifesting a belief in an optimistic outcome. It is the belief that once you replace negative thoughts with positive ones, you'll start having positive results. Norman Vincent Peale tells us, "Change your thoughts and you change your world. Believe in yourself. Have faith in your own abilities." Focusing on the positive rather than the negative, shapes our attitude, perspective and our ability to serve the elderly. Speak positively about yourself and what you can do. Do not entertain any negative thoughts or conversations that can bring you down. Lift your spirits up and you will invariable lift the spirits of others. James Truslow Adams is right, "The greatest discovery of my generation is that man can alter his life simply by altering his attitude." Keep a positive attitude as you serve aging adults. Encourage them and yourself.

PURPOSEFULNESS

Purposefulness is the quality of having excellent value or significance. It is someone who has a definite meaning and purpose in life. Ralph Waldo Emerson said, "The purpose of life is not to be happy. It is to be useful, to be honorable, to be compassionate, to have it make some difference that you have lived and lived well." The work that you do for aging adults is meaningful and extremely valuable. No institution can pay you enough for all the work that you do. However, take pride in the fact that you have made a major difference in someone's life. Never forget you are meant to live a life of passion and purpose. Someone once said, "If you cannot do what you want, learn to love what you do." Find joy and pride in your service to others.

PAMPER YOURSELF

Pampering yourself is very important to spiritual self-care. You must take time to love and care for yourself before you care for others. You cannot respect someone if you do not respect yourself. Therefore, you must begin to make yourself first on the priority list. Do things to make yourself feel good. Eat healthy food and exercise regularly. Listen to your favorite music. Occasionally go out to dinner and a movie. Enjoy your hobby. Spend quality time with a friend. Relax and alleviate stress in a bubble bath. Take a walk in the park and enjoy nature. Spend a romantic night with your spouse. Write a journal sharing all your thoughts and feelings. Go to Church and worship the Lord. You need to do what you can to make yourself feel better. Remember the wise words of my dear mother, *"Eat your dessert first."*

FINAL THOUGHTS

We have a choice. We could either age gracefully or age with sorrow in our heart, trouble in our mind and emptiness in our soul. It is up to you to have a positive attitude and embrace spiritual values which will transform and beautify your soul. **The secret to never growing old is keeping your soul new with love, hope, faith, peace, joy and grace.**

I hope that this book will assist you and others to age gracefully. Spiritual care for seniors is everyone's responsibility. We must use all our resources to help seniors to age gracefully. Sam Callow is right,

"The elderly are all someone's flesh and blood and we cannot just shut them in a cupboard and hand over the responsibility for taking care of them to the state." One of our top priorities should be caring for aging adults. As we learn to fit our busy lives around caring responsibilities for seniors, and the disabled, we will rediscover our spirituality. In fact, it is the height of spirituality to care for those persons who are unable to care for themselves. I pray that you age gracefully.

Notes

1. *Higher Stages of Consciousness.* Edited by C. N. Alexander and E.J. Langer. New York: Oxford University Press, 1990. Pages 286-341
2. "Becoming Wise." *International Journal of Aging and Human Development 32* (1991): 21-39.
3. Atchley, R.C. *Continuity and Adaptation in Aging.* Baltimore: John Hopkins University Press, 1999.
4. Thibault, J.M. *Aging as a Natural Monastery.* Aging and Spirituality 8 (1996): 3,8
5. Ferguson R (2011) George Mackay Brown: *The wound and the gift*, Edinburgh: St. Andrew Press
6. Koenig H. McCullough M and Larson D (2001) *Handbook of religion and health.* Oxford: Oxford University Press
7. David Moberg, 1971 Spirituality is difficult to define but there three common components (Bouchard, 1997)
8. King U (2011) *Can spirituality transform our world.* The Journal for the Study of Spirituality, 1, 17-34.
9. E.H. Erikson, *Dimensions of a New Identity*, Norton, New York, N.Y., USA, 1974.
10. White, Samuel., *It is Well with my Soul*, Indiana, Westbow Press. pg.1)
11. C.P. Hermann, *Spiritual needs of dying patients near the end of life are met, Oncology Nursing Forum*, vol.28, no. 1, pp. 67-72, 2001. View at Google Scholar View at Scopus
12. Ibid.
13. C. Dalbert, "Subjektives wohlbefinden junger erwachsener": *Zeitschrift fur Differetielle und Diagnostische Psychologie*, vol. 13, pp.207-220, 1992.
14. White, Samuel., *It is Well with my Soul*, pg.1, Indiana, Westbow Press.
15. White, Samuel, *It is Well with My Soul: Spiritual Care for the Dying*, pg. 1, Westbow Press
16. H.G. Koenig, H.J. Cohen, D.G. Blazer et al., *Religious coping and depression among elderly, hospitalized medically ill men, American Journal Psychiatry, vol.* 149, no.12, pp. 1693-1700, 1992. View at Google Scholar- View at Scopus
17. NHS Scotland, 2010:22

18. Richard Lewis, *Aging as a Spiritual Practice*
19. Mackinlay E and Trevitt *Living in aged care: Using spiritual reminiscence to enhance meaning in life for those with dementia*, International Journal of Mental Health Nursing, 19. 394-401)
20. Pulchaslski. C, *A time for listening and caring: spirituality and the care of the chronically ill and dying*, Oxford: Oxford University Press
21. Birren J and Schroots. J, (2006) *Autobiographical memory and the narrative self over the life span*, in J Birren and K Schaie (eds) Handbook of the psychology of aging, San Diego: Academic Press
22. Robertson-Gillam K (2008) *Hearing the voice of the elderly*: The potential for choir work to reduce depression and meet spiritual needs, in E Mackinlay (ed) Ageing, Disability and Spirituality: addressing the challenge of disability in later life, London: Jessica Kingsley
23. Goldsmith M (2004) *A strange land: People with dementia in the local church*, Southwell: 4M Publications
24. Speck P (1998) *Being There*, London: SCM Press
25. Mowat H (2004) *Successful ageing and the spiritual journey*, in A Jewel (ed) *Ageing spirituality and wellbeing*, London: Jessica Kingsley
26. White, Samuel, *It is Well with My Soul*, Westbow pg. 28-34)
27. Bishop Joe Pennel, Commentary: *Ministry of Presence is the most important gift*, December 25, 2012
28. White, Samuel, *It is well with My Soul*, Westbow Press pg.364)
29. White, Samuel, *It is Well with My Soul*, pg.364)
30. (Diane Schilling)
31. White, Samuel, *It is Well with My Soul*, Westbow Press. pg. 28
32. Life review Therapy Helps Alleviate Depression in the Elderly by Elements Behavioral Health posted on June 27, 2012 in Mood Disorders
33. Life Review Therapy Helps Alleviate Depression in the Elderly by Elements Behavioral Health posted on June 27, 2012 in Mood Disorders
34. White, Samuel, *It is Well with My Soul*, pg. 29, Westbow Press.
35. White, Samuel, *No More Tears*, pg.18, Westbow Press.
36. White, Samuel, *No More Tears*, pg.18,19, Westbow Press.
37. White, Samuel, *No More Tears*, pg.26, Westbow Press.
38. White, Samuel, *No More Tears*, pg. 43-54, Westbow Press
39. White, Samuel, *It is Well with My Soul*, pg.31, Westbow Press
40. White, Samuel, *It is Well with My Soul*, pg.33, Westbow Press.
41. White, Samuel, *It is Well with My Soul*, pg. 32, Westbow Press
42. Nursing Burnout, *Why it happens and what to do about it*, Kristina Ericksen, Rasmussen College
43. Nursing Burnout, *Why it happens and what to do about it*, Kristina Ericksen, Rasmussen College

Bibliography

Atchley A (2009) *Unraveling the mystery of health: how people manage stress and stay well*. San Francisco: Jossey- Bass

Atchley R (2009) *Spirituality and ageing*, Baltimore: John Hopkins University Press

Atchley, R.C. *Continuity and Adaptation in Aging*. Baltimore: John Hopkins University Press, 1999.

Birren J and Schroots J (2006) *Autobiographical memory and narrative self over the life span*, in J Birren and K Schaie (eds) Handbook of the psychology of aging, San Diego: Academic Press

Coleman P G (2011) *Belief and Ageing: spiritual pathways in later life*, Journal of Clinical Oncology, 23, 5520-5

C.P. Hermann, *The degree to which spiritual needs of patients near the end of life are met*, Oncology Nursing Forum, vol.34, no.1, pp. 70-78, 2007.

Caring for Your Aging Loved Ones (https://store.focusonthefamily.com/caring-for-your-aging-loved-ones

Complete Guide to Caring for Aging Loved Ones (https://store.focusonthe family.com/caring-for-your-aging-loved-ones

Erikson, E.H. Erikson, J.S. and Kivnick, H.Q. *Vital Involvement in Old Age*. New York: Norton, 1986.

Ferguson R (2001) George Mackay Brown, *The wound and the gift*, Edinburgh: St. Andrew Press

Frankl V (1984) *Man's search for meaning*, New York: Washington Square Press

G. Shea, *Meeting the pastoral care needs of an aging population*, Health Progress, vol.67, no.5, pp. 36-68, 1986.

Hall S, Longhurst S and Higginson I (2009) *Living and dying with dignity:*

A qualitative study of the views of older people in nursing homes, Aged and Ageing, 38, 411-416

Heelas P and Woodhead L (2005) *The spiritual revolution: why religion is giving way to spirituality*, Oxford: Blackwell Publishing

Jung C G (1970) Collected works (Volume 8), New Jersey: Princeton University Press

Kelly E (2012) *Personhood and presence: self as a resource for spiritual and pastoral care*, London: T and T Clark International

Kimble M (2000) *Victor Frankl's contribution to spirituality and ageing*, New York: Haworth Press

Koenig H (1994) *Aging and God: spiritual pathways to mental health in midlife and later years*, New York: The Haworth Pastoral Press

Lipe A (2002) *Beyond therapy: music, spirituality, and health in human experience- a review of the literature*, Journal of Music Therapy, 39, 209-240

Mackinlay E and Trevitt C (2010) *Living in aged care: Using spiritual reminiscence to enhance meaning in life for those with dementia*, International Journal of Mental Health Nursing, 19, 394-401

Mowat H (2004) *Successful ageing and the spiritual journey*, in a Jewell (ed) Ageing spirituality and wellbeing, London: Jessica Kingsley

Mowat H (2011) *Voicing the spiritual: Working with people with dementia*, London: Jessica Kingsley Publications

Moody, H.R. and Carrol, D. *The Five stages of the Soul*. New York: Anchor Books, 1997.

Moody, H.R., and Cole, T.R. (1986). *Aging and meaning: Bibliographic Essay*. In What Does it Mean to Grow Old? Edited by T.R. Cole and S. Gadow. Durham, N.C.: Duke University Press, 1986. Pages 247-253.

Nolan S (2012) *Spiritual care at the end of life: the chaplain as hopeful presence*, London: Jessica Kingsley

Pulchalski C (2006) *A time for listening and caring: spirituality and the care of the chronically ill and dying*, Oxford University press

Sheldrake P (2007) *A brief history of spirituality*. Oxford: Blackwell Publishing

Speck P (1988) *Being There*, London: SCM Press

Swinton J and Pattison S (2010) *Moving beyond clarity: Towards a thin, vague and useful understanding of spirituality in nursing care*

Thibault, J.M. : *Aging as a Natural Monastery, Aging and Spiritualty*(1996): pages 247- 253.
White, Samuel, *It is Well with My Soul*, Westbow Press, Indiana
White, Samuel, *No More Tears*, Westbow Press, Indiana.

Index

Aging Gracefully pg.69,70,80
Causes of Burn out/Self-Care pg.76
Clinical Spiritual Assessments pg.16,17
Caregiver Coping Skills pg.77
End of Life Care pg.19
Grief Counseling pg.42
Healing Cycle pg. 43
Multidimensional Spiritual Assessments pg.18,19,21-24
Natural Monastery pg.3
Religious seniors pg.6-9
Religious verses Spiritual pg.9,10
Spiritual Seniors pg.6
Spiritual
- needs pg.24,25
- tools pg.27-30
- interventions pg.31-42,45-47
- survey pg.50
- wellness topics pg.52-68
- coping skills pg.78
- values pg.69
- assessments pg.11

Appendix 1

Multidimensional Spiritual Assessment

1. Are you religious, spiritual or both?
2. If you are religious what is your religion and how does it help you?
3. What is your spiritual priority? On a scale of 1 to 3 and three represents your greatest need, what is *your* most important concern?

- **FAITH** – your beliefs, religion, spirituality, spiritual growth, coping skills, religious practices, closer to God, stronger faith, service to others, worship, prayer (1) (2) (3)
- **FEELINGS**- your sadness, loneliness, frustration, grief, depression, fears, guilt, anger, worry, want to learn how to experience: inner peace, joy, love for others, contentment, and love of self. (1) (2) (3)
- **FAMILY-** your relationships, reconciliation, forgiveness, conflict resolution, sharing your legacy, developing relationships (1) (2) (3)
- **FINANCE**- your material welfare, health concerns, food, shelter, clothing, debts (1) (2) (3)
- **FOCUS-** your goals, exploring your passions, hobbies or developing a new meaning and purpose in life (1) (2) (3)

- ***FAULTS*** – your moral failings, personal problems, coping with vices, addictions, unhealthy habits, forgiveness, guilt (1) (2) (3)
- ***FINITE*** - your death, funeral arrangements, Last Will & Testament, preparing for afterlife concerns about family (1) (2) (3)

4. If _____ represents your greatest spiritual need, how would you rate your ability to handle it? Larger numbers represent your ability to cope with your need. (1) (2) (3) (4) (5)

Appendix 2

Spiritual Care Needs Of Aging Adults

H.G. Koenig, H.J. Cohen, and D.G. Blazer developed the following spiritual care needs of the elderly. Once a need(s) are identified, a Social Worker can make a referral to the Chaplain for spiritual care services.

- Need for support in dealing with loss
- Need to transcend circumstances
- Need to be forgiven and to forgive
- Need to find meaning and purpose
- Need to love and serve other
- Need for unconditional love
- Need to feel that God is on their side
- Need to be thankful
- Need to prepare for death and dying
- Need for continuity
- Need for validation and support of religious behaviors
- Need for personal dignity and sense of worthiness
- Need to express feelings: anger, sadness, despair, doubt, fear, guilt, confusion, anxiety, boredom, meaninglessness etc.
- Need to feel loved, respected and appreciated
- Need to give love, serve, feel useful, share, pass on legacy

- Need to grow spiritually and or emotionally
- Need to address faults, vices, addictions, mistakes in the past and weaknesses

"Religious coping and depression among elderly, hospitalized medically ill men," *American Journal of Psychiatry*, vol. 149, no. 12, pp. 1693-1700, 1992. View at Google Scholar-View at Scopus

Appendix 3

Different Religious Beliefs And Practices

It is important to understand an elderly person's religion, especially if we are going to care for their spiritual needs. We do not have to believe in each other's religion, but we must respect a person's right to practice it. These brief summaries of Islam, Jehovah Witnesses, Judaism and Catholicism can begin the process of understanding and lay the ground work for spiritual care. Further research in each of these religions is necessary to fully understand their beliefs and practices.

ISLAM

The Arabic word "Islam" means "submission" and derives from a word meaning "peace." Islam is a complete submission to the will of God. It is both a religion and a complete way of life of peace, mercy, and forgiveness. The prophet Muhammad (SAW) was born in Makkah in the year 570 and at 40 received his first revelation from God through the Angel Gabriel. This revelation is known as the Quran and it is the exact unchanged Word of Allah to all humankind. Muslims believe that Allah sent Messengers to each nation throughout the history of humankind. Messengers came with the same message: to worship the One Supreme God and to obey His Commands. Islam emphasizes a Belief in Allah, His Angels, the Day of Judgement, Destiny and His Prophets and Messengers (Five prominent divine books are: Abraham's Scrolls;

Zabor(Psalm) revealed to Prophet David; Tawrah (Torah) revealed to Prophet Moses; Inji (Gospel) revealed to Prophet Jesus; Quran revealed to Prophet Muhammed.

There are five pillars of Islam: (1) *Shahada* (Testify) (2) *Salah* (Prayer) five specific times a day: Dawn, Noon, Afternoon, Sunset, and Night. A ritual cleaning called Wudu is a prerequisite to Salah. (3*) Seyam* (Fasting) is during the month of Ramadan and it is an obligation for every healthy Muslim. Fasting is total abstinence from eating, drinking, smoking, gum, intimate relations, and taking anything into the body. The ill are exempt from fasting. (4) *Zakat* (Charity) is an annual obligatory charity on every Muslim to support workers. (5*) Hajj* (Pilgrimage) It is a spiritual journey required of all Muslims to travel to Makkah and devote all their attention to Allah alone.

- **CARE OF ELDERLY** - Islam has given the elderly a special status as there are texts which urge Muslims to respect and honor them. The Prophet said: "Part of glorifying Allaah is honoring the grey-haired Muslim." The Prophet warned, "He is not one of us who does not show mercy to our young ones and respect our old ones." There are several ways Muslims care for the elderly:
  1. Enjoining effective treatment of parents. A part of Worshipping Allah is caring and honoring parents. [al-Nisa' 4:36]
  2. Enjoining honoring one's parents' friends even after the parents have passed away, and regarding that as part of honoring one's parents. This ensures the memories of the deceased parent and decreases the sense of isolation and loneliness of the elderly.

- **DEATH IS IMMINENT-** When a Muslim is approaching death all family members and close friends will be present. They will offer the dying person "shahada" confirming that there is no God but Allah. When death has occurred, those present will say, "Inna lillahi wa inna ilayhi raji'un" (Verily we belong to Allah, and truly to Him shall we return"). Those present will close the deceased eyes and lower jaw and cover the body with a clean sheet. They will make a "dua" (supplication) to Allah to forgive sins of the deceased.

JEHOVAH WITNESS

Jehovah Witness was established in 1879 and their beliefs are found in the *New World Translation of the Holy Scriptures*. Jehovah Witness basic beliefs are:

1. *God.* He is the Creator, whose name is Jehovah (Psalm 83:18; Revelation 4:11) He is the God of Abraham, Moses, and Jesus.
2. *Bible.* They accept all 66 books of the Bible and believe that parts of the Bible were written in figurative or symbolic language and not understood literally
3. *Jesus.* They follow the teachings of Christ as the Son of God. They do not believe that Jesus is God or believe in a Holy trinity.
4. *The Kingdom of Heaven.* This is a real government in heaven, that will replace human governments in "the last days."
5. *Salvation.* Deliverance from sin and death is through the ransom sacrifice of Jesus
6. *Heaven.* Jehovah God, Jesus Christ, the angels and 144,00 will be resurrected to life in heaven to rule with Jesus in the Kingdom
7. *Earth.* God created the earth to be humankinds eternal home, an earthly paradise.
8. *Evil and suffering.* These began when one of God's angels Satan rebelled and persuaded the first human couple to join him and this created evil and suffering.
9. Death. God will bring billions back from death by means of a resurrection and if they refuse to learn God's ways they will be destroyed.
10. *Family.* They believe that marriage is between a man and a woman and adultery is the only grounds for divorce.
11. Worship. They do not venerate the cross or any other images. They pray, study Bible, meditate on the Bible, preach the "good news of the Kingdom", help the needy, build Kingdom halls, and share in disaster relief.

12. *Organization.* They are organized into congregations which is overseen by a body of elders who are unsalaried. They do not practice tithing or take up offerings. All activities are supported by anonymous donations. The Governing Body, a small group of elders who serve at their world headquarters, provide direction for all Jehovah Witnesses.
13. *Unity.* They are united in their beliefs and work hard to have no social, ethnic, racial, or class divisions.
14. *Conduct.* They strive to show unselfish love in all their actions. They refuse taking blood transfusions (Acts 15:28,29; Galatians 5:19-21) They respect the government but refuse to pledge allegiance, vote, or volunteer for armed services.
15. *Relationship with others.* They are guided by the *Golden Rule,* however they try to remain neutral in political affairs, avoid affiliating with other religions, do not participate in Easter, Christmas and other worldly celebrations.

- **CARE OF THE ELDERLY**- Jehovah witness believe that caring for the elderly is a Christian responsibility. (Isaiah 46:4; Psalm 48:14; Ephesians 6:2; Exodus 20:12)
- **DEATH OF A JEHOVAH WITNESS**- they believe that the soul waits, in an unconscious state, for resurrection to life. The Jehovah Witnesses funeral service is similar to other Christian faiths but is a very brief service focusing on Jehovah Witness teachings.

JUDAISM

Judaism's founders were Abraham and Moses. Judaism promulgates monotheism, that there is only one God: Yahew (YHVH) who chose the people of Israel. Only God created the universe and only He controls it. God is one, whole, complete being.

Beliefs- Yahew chose the people of Israel and who requires worship, ethical behavior and rituals. A Messiah will come.

Practices- circumcision at birth, bar/ bat mitzvah at adulthood, observing sabbath by worshipping at the Synagogue, wearing tallit and tefillin, prayer services, eating only "kosher" foods and abstaining from pork, shellish, and any meat that has not been ritually slaughtered

Main Holidays- Hanukkah, Rosh Hashanah, Purim

Texts- Hebrew Bible (Tanakh); Talmud

Symbols – Star of David, chai, hamsa, tree

CARING FOR THE ELDERLY- Jewish culture and religion promotes the care of the elderly. Louis J. Novick writes, "The responsibility of offspring to their parents, which is expressed in honoring them, supporting them financially when they require it and the children have the means to supply it, and being physically present when such presence is necessary so to sustain the emotional health of parents, it is a basic tenet of Jewish ethics. When aged parents require a level of care that their children cannot themselves provide, seeking admission to a good long-term facility may fulfill the imperative of the Fifth Commandment, 'Honor your father and mother." The scriptures admonish us, "You shall honor the old." (Leviticus 19:32) "Remember the days long gone by. Ponder the years of each generation. Ask your father and let him tell you, and your grandfather, who will explain it." (Deuteronomy 32:7) Finally, Rabbi Nachman of Breslav said, "Gauge a country's prosperity by its treatment of the aged."

CARING FOR THE DYING- Encourage family and friends to come over to share their support. A rabbi may need to visit to hear their confession (viddui) and pray with them. Also, family may need to talk to rabbi about living wills, life support, ceasing medical care, and Jewish Hospice care. After the burial, the bereaved will mourn for a seven-day "Shivah" to the 30-day *shloshim* period. Mourning is a sign of respect to the deceased and crucial to the healing process.

CATHOLICISM

Christians believe that Jesus Christ is the Son of God and was crucified, died, buried and resurrected and those who believe in him will have eternal life. Catholics believe the following:

Bible- is the inspired, error-free, and revealed word of God

Baptism- the rite of becoming a Christian, is necessary for salvation. Catholics believe in infant Baptism, sprinkling and immersion.

God's Ten Commandments provide a moral compass and an ethical standard to live by

Holy Trinity- is the belief in one God in three persons, God the Father, God the Son and God the Holy Spirit.

Catholic practices- celebrate their faith in a wide variety of ways based on regional culture and ethnicity. Some Catholics practice the Sacrament: Penance, fasting & abstinence, Mass and Spiritual Communion, Eucharistic Adoration, Stations of the Cross, Consecration to Jesus through Mary, The Rosary: Mary's Psalter, Morning Offering, The 6 Approved Litanies, Novenas, The Signs of the Cross, Veiling, Posture and Gesture, Lectio Divina and Traditional Prayers, Creeds, and Ejaculations.

CARE FOR ELDERLY / TERMINALLY ILL

When a Catholic is bed-ridden, homebound, or in the hospital, the priest will visit and offer the Eucharist, hear the Confession, Extreme Unction or Anointing of the Sick. The Last Rites can only be administered by a priest or bishop or what is called the Anointing of the Sick. The purpose of the Anointing of the Sick is to give comfort and spiritual healing to the ill or dying. In the absence of the priest the Anointing of the Sick can not be ministered by a lay person. A Lay person can give Holy Communion.

Appendix 4

Spiritual Care Plan

A Spiritual Care Plan summarizes the care to be given to the terminally and their family. It is a set of a spiritual actions that help to address the elderly persons symptoms, aims and measured outcomes. It is a guide used to evaluate the effectiveness of the spiritual care rendered. Every spiritual care plan will include the elderly persons *Symptoms, Aims,* and *Measurement* that can be summarized in an acrostic called S. A. M.

S – Is for Symptoms or the primary concerns of the elderly. Some of these symptoms or concerns are: family, feelings, focus, faults, and finite being. The elderly may manifest spiritual illnesses like toxic guilt, sadness, meaninglessness, anger, despair, alienation, and hopelessness. Whatever the spiritual symptom or need should be recognized and addressed by the aged and the spiritual care provider.

A – Is for Aim or goal of the elderly person. The aim must be patient specific, or client centered. The aim is always patient, or family driven. It is not the goal of the spiritual care provider. The aim is the realistic expectation of the senior. It's what they want or hope for. The spiritual care provider will render spiritual interventions to assist the patient to fulfill their aim.

M – is for measuring the outcome. Measuring the outcome of the aim will determine the effectiveness of the spiritual care plan. The senior is asked for their level of satisfaction using a scale from 1 to 5.

The higher the number the greater the satisfaction with their ability to cope with their spiritual need.

SPIRITUAL CARE PLAN

Symptom – What is the spiritual need?
Aim – What is your goal? What is it that you want to accomplish?
Measurement – How do you rate your ability to cope with your need? (1 to 5)

"Gone From My Sight"

Appendix 5

Spiritual Care for Persons with Dementia

My eighty-three-year-old mother was frantic when she asked me, "Do you know what happened to my car? Did someone steal it? Did one of you kids borrow it and take it somewhere? Where is my car? Help me find it!"

We walked out to the parking lot of her assisted living residence searching for her car. Tragically, my mother forgot that she had sold her car ten years ago. This was the first time that I witnessed my mother with dementia.

We walked all around the parking lot looking for a car that no longer existed. She pointed out a car, I would look at it and we'd continue our search. We searched for her car until she got tired and wanted to go back to her room.

I was emotionally drained watching my mother walk aimlessly through the parking lot. It was heart wrenching seeing her mind deteriorate like that. Dementia had changed her and subsequently, challenged my level of care. There was so much I did not know about the dementia and Alzheimer's. What are the various symptoms and behaviors of persons with this debilitating disease and what can we do to help them?

How do clergy, caregivers and spiritual care persons render spiritual care to persons losing their cognitive abilities? What spiritual interventions are needed to give them peace and comfort? What can a clergy person or caregiver do to support the family as they care for their loved ones?

I am thankful for Ms. Teepa Snow, MS, OTR/L, FAOTA who brilliantly developed *THE LIVING GEMS* model to recognize the dynamic nature of the human brain and its abilities. Unlike other cognitive models, it acknowledges that everyone's abilities can change in a moment. Modifying environments, situations, interactions, and expectations will create either supportive positive opportunities or result in distress and a sense of failure. Just as gems need different settings and care to show their best characteristics, so do people. Rather than focus on a person's loss when there is a brain change, seeing individuals as precious, unique, and capable encourages a care partnership and is the core of this model. Providing supportive settings for everyone, including care providers, allows them to use what they have to be their best. The GEMS advocate that everyone living with brain change when given the opportunity will shine. **Teepa Snow and Positive Approach to Care Team**

SENIOR GEMS STRATEGY FOR CARE

I. SAPPHIRE – Normal Aging

Basic Characteristics- feel sad because of changes due to normal aging, can learn new things, repetition is needed, ability to take in information is slowing, making decisions can take extra time

Strategies that Work- respecting their choices and decisions, noticing and checking out changes in emotional or physical well-being, using written reinforcements (calendar, notes, lists), using validation and empathy

Strategies to Avoid- telling instead of asking, arguing or not honoring choices, asking for quick decisions on important matters, being bossy, taking over without permission.

Spiritual Care Intervention- affirm the fact that God is with them as they experience the aging process. Clergy and caregiver recommended interventions:

- Remind them of the love of God that cares for them as they endure the changes and losses of the aging process.

- Recite comforting scriptures
- Remind them to have faith in God and in themselves to make the right decisions for themselves. (Philippians 4:13)
- Encourage Life Review and validate their accomplishments and experiences
- Discuss with family the symptoms of Alzheimer's and Dementia
- Discuss with patient, family, social worker the need for *Medical Power of Attorney* to make health decisions on behalf of patient when they are unable to make decisions. Offer to be a family mediator.
- Discuss with patient, family, social worker the need for a *Durable Power of Attorney* who will make financial and legal decisions on behalf of patient when they are unable to make decisions. Offer to be a family mediator.

II. DIAMOND- *Early-Stage Dementia*

Basic Characteristics- uses old habits and routines, becomes more protective of self and belongings, less aware of boundaries, likes things that are familiar and has difficulty with change, may share old stories and ask questions repeatedly

Strategies that Work- offering apologies, approaching and speaking as a friend, not authority, using the phrase, "We could try", using established habits and routines when possible, going with their flow, giving up being "Right"

Strategies to Avoid- using the phrase "Don't you remember?", not accepting changing abilities, robbing them of opportunities to participate, not offering alternative responsibilities when taking over tasks, forcing changes or arguing

Spiritual Care Intervention - remind them that God is with them during life's changes and confusion. Clergy and caregiver can render the following services:

- Render *ministry of presence* and assist them in their daily routine
- Encourage them share their life stories and affirm their past

- Be patient and understanding as you introduce change. Remind them that God is with them as life changes. God states, "Behold, I am doing a new thing, do you not perceive it?" (Isaiah 43:19)
- Reintroduce or affirm their hobbies or passions
- Look at picture album and talk about "the good old days."
- Reframe negative circumstances into positive ones
- Encourage flexibility - with every reversal comes a new opportunity
- Careful Listening gives them a sense of hope, meaning and purpose

III. EMERALD- *Early to Mid-Stage Dementia*

Basic Characteristics- may lose their personal timeline of past life, places, and roles, emotions change quickly, may misplace important things and accuse others of taking belongings, words are vague or not on target, ability to comprehend is limited

Strategies that Work- correcting mistakes discreetly, getting connected to the person prior to doing tasks or care, presenting one step at a time, using humor, doing tasks together, greeting before you treat

Strategies to Avoid- pointing out all of their errors, putting your hands on them without proper cues, treating them as children, using reality orientation, lying to them when they become confused, acting bossy.

Spiritual Care Intervention - remind them that God is with them and will take care of them. Clergy and caregiver can address their feelings of insecurity and vulnerability by doing the following:

- Reciting scriptures of the presence of God.
- Exhibit the grace and patience of God as you assist them.
- Remind them that God is with them in their daily tasks.
- Point out to life's blessings and accentuate the positive.
- Remind family to be patient and understanding
- Enter "their world" and helping them find peace
- Gently encourage them to be flexible, to let go and let God.
- Empathetic listening

- If they are unable to attend Church, create a simple worship service in their room (Invocation, Scripture reading, song, brief meditation, and closing prayer) Or, watch or listen to religious programs

IV. AMBER-Mid-Stage Dementia

Basic Characteristics- seeks enjoyable sensory experiences (hearing music, soft blanket), gets into things, difficult to communicate needs, may be private and quiet, or public and loud, in the moment, can't wait

Strategies that Work- demonstrating or showing what you want them to do, limiting distractions, communicating with tone of voice, facial expression, and props or objects, building in time away from each other, approach, back off, then re-approach when something isn't working

Strategies to Avoid- using lots of explanations or words, doing to them or for them instead of with them, not having permission to do tasks, being loud, allowing too much stimulation, trying to complete tasks when distressed

Spiritual Care Intervention- ministry of presence is essential. Clergy and caregiver can do the following:

- Be in the moment. Whatever they need, if it is possible, give it to them.
- Playing their favorite music can stimulate their memory and put em in a good mood.
- Assist them in daily chores or activities
- Reveal the love of God with a pleasant demeanor, soft tone of voice and positive attitude, and gracious spirit
- Holding hands and praying together
- Watching T.V. together
- Assisting them in playing Bingo and other games or activities
- Listening to the feeling behind their incoherent speech
- If they are unable to attend Church, create a simple worship service in their room.

V. RUBY-Mid to Late-Stage Dementia

Basic Characteristics- big movements and strength in arms and legs remain, but skilled use of fingers, feet, eyes, and mouth are lost, can do only one thing at a time (look, listen, rest), may put or hold food in their mouth, but not safely chew or swallow it.

Strategies that Work- using rhythm and music more than words and speech, using demonstration more than gestures or instructions, slowing down, take more time to get them to notice you, get connected before starting a task

Strategies to Avoid- trying to get tasks done quickly or make them do it with force or pressure, giving too many pieces of information or options at a time, going fast, using high pitched tone of voice or "baby talk."

Spiritual Care Intervention- render ministry of presence by participating in daily activities. Clergy and caregiver can do the following:

- Sit, hold their hand, be physically and emotionally present. You do not have to say or do anything, just be prayerful. Your presence speaks louder than words.
- After getting permission from the health care provider, assisting them with their meal.
- Reading comforting scriptures to them
- Praying with and for them
- Play their favorite music
- Assist patient with Activities of Daily Living
- If they are unable to attend Church, create a simple worship service in their room.

VI. PEARL-Last Stage Dementia

Basic Characteristics- able to connect with the world around them for short periods of time, spends most time inside themselves, takes a long time for information/data from the world to be taken in and processed, startles easily with unexpected movement, touch, or other sensations

Strategies that Work- taking time to look at the person, listen to them, and notice what it is happening before you start to care, using a soothing tone and rhythmic voice, offering comfort through preferred touch, rhythm, and sight options

Strategies to Avoid- hurrying through movements to get tasks done, worrying more about the body than the person living inside it, forgetting to let the person know you are there before you start to do things, talking about the person, not <u>to</u> the person

Spiritual Care Intervention - render ministry of presence and do what ever you can to make them feel comfortable. Spending a lot of time helping family to cope with loss and the inevitability of death. Clergy and caregiver can use the following interventions:

- Ministry of presence
- Reading scriptures, and praying for them
- Comforting the family as they witness the radical changes in their loved one. Helping them to understand and accept the symptoms of the disease and not take it personal
- Assisting patient with Activities of Daily Living
- Praying with and for the family and caregivers
- Offering anticipatory grief counseling to prepare family for death and loss
- Encourage primary caregiver and family to take care of themselves.
- Gather family around the bedside of patient, read a comforting scripture and have them hold hands as you pray for patient.

The source of this information is derived from **www.Teepa Snow.com**

The Spiritual Care Interventions are derived from Dr. Samuel White III's sixteen years of Hospice Chaplaincy and thirty years of pastoral care.

Appendix 6

Aging Gracefully Session

WHY:
All aging adults have spiritual needs that should be addressed. Many are struggling with loneliness, apathy, meaninglessness, spiritual emptiness, grief, hopelessness, love, joy and sense of their mortality.

WHAT:
The purpose of the *Aging Gracefully Sessions* is to address the elderly persons spiritual needs and to help them to age gracefully. Aging gracefully is the transformation and beautification of the soul through discussion and application of universal values and spiritual concepts. The goal is to encourage staff and participants to engage in a lively discussion that will foster self-improvement.

The Aging Gracefully Session is not a religious activity or a Bible Study. No particular religion should be promulgated or diminished. Staff and participants are encouraged to share their feelings and beliefs but not proselytize.

WHO:
PACE staff and aging adults are encouraged to expound their thoughts and feelings. Aging Gracefully Session will be facilitated by Spiritual Care Coordinator or staff.

WHERE:
Aging Gracefully Session can be held at each PACE day health center or designated area.

WHEN:
Director, manager or Spiritual Care Coordinator can schedule an Aging Gracefully Session once per month. Each session will generally take about a half an hour to an hour depending on the interest level of the aging adults.

HOW: Staff will distribute Aging Gracefully Session worksheet to all participants. There should not be any other games or activities going on. We will reserve a room for participants who do not want to participate. Spiritual Care person or designee can explain the purpose of the Aging Gracefully Session and encourage everyone to share their thoughts and feelings. Try not let anyone monopolize the group discussion. Keep the conversation going and add questions if necessary. The goal is to get everyone talking and reflecting on how they can improve themselves.

The Aging Gracefully Sessions are derived from the book, *Aging Gracefully: Spiritual Care for Aging Adults* by Dr. Samuel White, III

Aging Gracefully Session

Extraordinary Care is a PACE value that is applicable to staff and participants. Extraordinary care is displaying kindness and care consistently. We age gracefully when we are kind, actively listen, anticipate the needs of others, offer help and engage with friendliness and warmth.

DISCUSSION QUESTIONS:

- Recall a time in your life when you exhibited extraordinary care? (Raise children, grandchildren, military service, etc.)
- What PACE staff gives you extraordinary care?
- How can you give extraordinary care to others?
- How can you give extraordinary care to yourself?
- Share an example of someone being kind or caring to you?
- What could our PACE staff do to show you extraordinary care?

Aging Gracefully Session

Collaborative Teamwork is a PACE value that is applicable to staff and participants. Collaborative Teamwork means including, appreciating and working with others despite differences. We age gracefully when we treat everyone with respect, open to differences, forgive, listen, communicate and work in harmony.

DISCUSSION QUESTIONS:

- What are some of the things that prevent people from working together?
- What should you do when you have a disagreement?
- Why is forgiving someone good for your body and soul?
- Why is it important to communicate your thoughts and feelings?
- What is the difference between listening and hearing?
- What can a participant do to collaborate with the bus driver, CNA, physical therapist, nurse, social worker, and physician?
- What could the PACE staff do to show collaborative teamwork?

Aging Gracefully Session

Inspired Achievement is a PACE value that staff, and participant can share. Inspired Achievement means to strive to do your best work every day and do more than what is expected. A part of aging gracefully is appreciating your strengths, skills and experiences and using them to the best of your ability.

DISCUSSION QUESTIONS:

- What are your talents, skills, abilities?
- Share some of your accomplishments, or achievements.
- What are you most proud of and why?
- What or who inspires you?
- What are your goals or dreams? What do you want to do?
- What could you do to improve your life?
- What can PACE staff do to inspire or encourage achievement in participants?

Aging Gracefully Session

Accountability is a PACE value that participant and staff should practice. Accountability means mutual respect and support. We express our gratitude and recognize the contributions of others. Also, we are direct, honest, and respectful in conversation; giving and receiving feedback. We age gracefully when we hold each other accountable.

DISCUSSION QUESTIONS:

- What are some things you could say do to hold the staff accountable?
- Someone once said, "It is not what you say, but how you say it." What does this mean?
- Why is it difficult to give honest feedback?
- Why is it difficult to receive honest feedback?
- Why is accountability an important value?
- What happens when you don't hold people accountable?
- What could the PACE staff do to encourage accountability?

Aging Gracefully Session

Adaptive Growth is a PACE value that means to evolve, keep learning and adapting as you grow. If we want to age gracefully, we must be willing to learn new things, behaviors, attitudes and ideas. We should always be willing to educate ourselves.

DISCUSSION QUESTIONS:

- Why are people resistant to change?
- What happens to people who refuse to change or learn anything new?
- What do you want to change at PACE?
- What do you want to change in yourself?
- The death of a loved one is a major change; how do you cope with it?
- The loss of your health, wealth and independence is a difficult change, how do you handle it?
- What new ideas, skills, and behaviors have you learned?
- How can PACE change to improve itself?

Aging Gracefully Session

Subject: Love

It has been said that the greatest commandment is, "Thou shalt love the Lord thy God with all thy heart, and all thy soul, and with all thy mind. And thy neighbor as yourself." (Matthew 22:37) There is nothing more powerful than love. Love can transform a foe into a friend, heal a broken heart and bring joy to the soul. Thomas Merton once wrote, "Love seeks one thing only: the good of the one loved. It leaves all the other secondary effects to take care of themselves. Love, therefore, is its own reward."

DISCUSSION QUESTIONS:

- Why is it so important to love people?
- Why is it important to love God?
- Why is it important to love yourself?
- What are somethings you could to love yourself?
- What are somethings you could to love God?
- What are somethings that you could to love others

Aging Gracefully Session

Subject: Hope

Bishop Desmond Tutu once said, "Hope is being able to see the light despite all of the darkness." When a person loses hope they find it difficult to see goodness in themselves, in people and in the world. They tend to focus on the negative instead of the positive. One of the ways we keep a sense of hope is by looking past the darkness of despair to see the light of hope.

DISCUSSION QUESTIONS:

- What are some good things you see happening in the world or at PACE?
- Share some positive experience or "testify" about the goodness of God.
- What gives you hope and why?
- What do you do when you are sad? How do you cheer yourself up?
- Some people say, "the glass is half empty and others say the glass is half full." What do you say?
- What else could we do to make our PACE center a positive experience?

Aging Gracefully Session

Subject: Happiness

Abraham Lincoln said, "People are as happy as they want to be." In other words, happiness is a choice, it is a positive attitude. Happiness is positive perspective, emphasizing good instead of evil; hope instead of despair. It is up to you to decide if you want to be happy. No one or nothing can upset you unless you let them. You must make a conscious decision to be happy.

DISCUSSION QUESTIONS:

- What can you do to make yourself happy?
- How does negative thinking or a bad attitude impact your life?
- What or who makes you happy?
- How can you bring happiness to others?
- What can we do to make our PACE center a positive, joyful experience?

Aging Gracefully Session

Subject: Stroll Down Memory Lane

The poet Loretta Hitch wrote a poem called, "Stroll Down Memory Lane." She reminds us that we need to reflect on the past and learn to appreciate all the experiences of our life. Our memories represent our identity, history, culture, social and personal experiences. *Taking a stroll down memory lane* can counteract loneliness, boredom, hopelessness and foster a sense of gratitude, peace and self-affirmation.

DISCUSSION QUESTIONS:

- What is your favorite memory?
- What is your favorite old movie, music group, entertainer, song, or T.V. show and why?
- What memory brings a smile to your face?
- What kind of a childhood or parents did you have?
- What is your favorite high school memory?
- Tell us about your "good old days."

Aging gracefully Session

Subject: Carpe Diem

The Roman poet Horace used the Latin expression, Carpe Diem. It literally means "Pluck the Day" and is translated "Seize the Day." In other words, we must make the most of our present time. We must live ever day as if it were our last. We should not procrastinate or take life for granted. Do not wait for something to happen, make it happen. We age gracefully when we make the most out of life.

DISCUSSION QUESTIONS:

- What happens when we procrastinate?
- Why do people take life for granted?
- What do you need to do before you die?
- What do you need to do to enjoy your life?
- If you knew you were going to die next week, what would you do differently?
- How can we make our PACE center a celebration of life?

Aging Gracefully Session

Subject: Aging Gracefully

The immortal movie actress Bette Davis is right, "Old age is not for the weak." As we get older, we face more physical, emotional, financial, psychological and spiritual challenges. Despite our losses and challenges, we can still age gracefully. Aging gracefully is the transformation and beautification of the soul through acceptance and application of spiritual values. Aging gracefully is an inside job of the heart, mind and soul. It means to cultivate a positive attitude and resilient spirit. We cannot stop the challenges of getting old, however, we can determine how we respond to them. We age gracefully when we respond positively to life's losses.

DISCUSSION QUESTIONS:

- What does it mean to you to age gracefully?
- What kind of attitude do you need to deal with life's challenges and losses?
- How do you overcome adversity?
- What can our PACE center do to help the elderly to age gracefully?

CPSIA information can be obtained
at www.ICGtesting.com
Printed in the USA
FSHW011128050220
66826FS